TAGINE COOKBOOK

TOP HEALTHY AND DELICIOUS MOROCCAN TAGINE RECIPES

ABDUL AZIZ

Copyright © 2021 by Abdul Aziz

All rights reserved.

No part of this book may be reproduced in any form or by any electronic or mechanical means, including information storage and retrieval systems, without written permission from the author, except for the use of brief quotations in a book review.

CONTENTS

Introduction   v

1. What Is A Tagine?   1
2. How Does Tagine Work?   14
3. How To Use A Tagine   22
4. What Beginner Chefs Need to Appreciate Concerning Cooking with Tagine   28
5. How to Prepare the Top Healthy Delicious Moroccan Tagine Recipes   35

Conclusion   209

INTRODUCTION

Home chefs always search for new ideas in cooking or methods to serve their dishes. A method which quite many amateur chefs may have never heard of is tagine cooking. Tagine food is so named since earthenware pots are usually used. These pots are often circular containers covered by a big domed lid. This way of cooking is commonly found in Moroccan cuisine.

Introduction

There are two common types of tagines, i.e., cooking and serving. They are the same except that the serving type is usually glazed and painted in color. Traditionally, tagine cooking was done by burning charcoal, and stews consisting of lamb, fish, and chicken were often cooked.

Tagine became more and more popular because it requires a minimal amount of water, which was scarce at its place of origin. Besides, even though the food inside is cooked for many hours, the covered lid helps keep the moisture and juice inside. And the flavor of oil and spices could infuse into the food thoroughly.

In the tagine, it may be uneasy about buying a nice tagine. Nowadays, tagines could be found in mage stores and home accessory stores alongside cookware. You can even find them on Amazon. There are a variety of tagines with different sizes and styles. The price could be as cheap as $20 or as expensive as $100 or more.

Like how you buy other cookware, budget and personal choice always come into consideration. Anyhow, please note that nowadays, most tagines are serving types. You will need to spend some time researching the market if you want an authentic cooking type tagine (which you don't necessarily need to buy).

Before you cook the food, you need to prepare your tagine. The simplest way to do this is to soak the tagine in water for a few hours (you can place it in a washing sink). After that, dry the tagine and coat the base's interior and the lid with a thin coat of olive oil. You need to put it in an unheated oven before you raise the temperature to around 320 degrees. Fahrenheit. Remove the tagine from the oven 2 hours later, allow it to cool down. Coat the tagine with another coat of olive oil. Now you can store your tagine before using it for the first time.

With a proper oven, the overall cooking time is 30 to 40 minutes, making tagine cooking an easy thing to do. Tagines are quite durable; if you properly use and wash your tagine, they should be able to serve you for many years to come.

Do You Need a Tagine?

Even if you've never been to Morocco or tried their food, you might find that a tagine forever changes your cooking. As they can be used in a similar way to a Dutch oven, which retains heat for hours and enables slow cooking, there is an incredible versatility of dishes that can be made with this device. Electric slow cookers are expensive, and tagines produce similar dishes - with the added endorsement that they have been used for centuries in traditional Moroccan cooking!

Suppose you are keen to try some authentic Moroccan dishes and have a slow cooker to make various meals for all tastebuds. In that case, you may find yourself to be hugely benefited by getting a tagine!

In this book, you'll understand that cooking with a tagine is definitely a fun process. And since it's not so difficult, many amateur cooks would find using tagine enjoyable. If you've been lured into purchasing a Moroccan tagine for the first time and wonder what delicious dishes can be made in its cone-shaped ceramic vessel—you've come to the right place. This traditional cookware is ideal for rich, slow-cooked stews of meat, poultry, or fish and makes a perfect one-pot meal to share at a dinner party.

1

WHAT IS A TAGINE?

A TAGINE SOMETIMES SPELLED "TAJINE," IS A TRADITIONAL Moroccan cooking vessel made of ceramic or unglazed clay with a round base and low sides. A cone-shaped cover sits on the base during cooking. The conical lid traps steam during cooking and returns the liquid to the clay pot, resulting in a moist dish with concentrated flavors.

Tagine is also the name for a Maghrebi, or North African, a dish cooked in the tagine pot. Tagine is closely associated with Moroccan cuisine, where slow-cooked savory stews made with meat, poultry, or fish, are cooked with vegetables, aromatic spices, dried fruit, and nuts.

Usually, a tagine is referred to as an item on a menu. Tagine is the cookware itself. It's a two-piece clay pot used to make a dish like

Chicken Tagine. The reason for using a tagine is to make a dish tender and bring out its natural flavors.

The unique shape of the tagine, with fluted cone tops, allows for it to trap steam as the dish cooks. This allows the dish to be cooked inside evenly. Originally, Tagines were used in North America for making food over the fire.

The History of Tagine

The tagine dates back to Harun al Rashid, who was a ruler of the Islamic empire. Some sources date it back to the Roman Empire because of the portable ovens used by Romans that are similar to tagines.

Moroccan influences over the years are what makes the tagine unique. Recipes have evolved, and many spices have been introduced to Moroccan culture while using the tagine for cooking well-known recipes.

. . .

A tagine is an important part of Moroccan cuisine and has been a part of the culture for hundreds of years. The word tagine has two meanings. First, it refers to North African cookware traditionally made of clay or ceramic. The bottom is a wide, shallow circular dish used for cooking and serving, while the top of the tagine is distinctively shaped into a rounded dome or cone.

Second, the word tagine also refers to the succulent, stew-like dish slow-cooked in the traditional cookware. Typically, a tagine is a rich mixture of meat, poultry, or fish and most often includes vegetables or fruit. Vegetables may also be cooked alone in the tagine.

Most people agree that the tagine's origin dates back to the late 18th century when Harun al Rashid ruled the Islamic Empire. However, another school of thought that the use of ceramics in Moroccan cooking is probably of Roman influence; Romans were known for their ceramics and likely brought that tradition to their rule of Roman Africa. Either way, the first appearance of recipes cooked tagine-style appeared in the 9th century in the publication The Thousand and One Nights.

. . .

Tagine the Vessel

Today, ceramic tagines are practical yet exquisite examples of Moroccan artisanship, and many are showpieces and functional cooking vessels. Some tagines, however, are intended only to be used as decorative serving dishes.

The cooking vessel is made of clay or ceramic (although some Western cookware companies are now making tagines from other materials) and can be left as is or coated in a glaze. Many cooks favor unglazed clay tagines for the unique earthy nuance they impart to dishes. Tagines come in all sizes; the smallest might hold enough food for one or two people, while the largest can hold a meal for eight people or more.

The purpose of the dome- or cone-shaped top is to return moisture to the base of the tagine, creating a moist and flavorful dish.

Tagine the Stew

Tagines are primarily used to slow-cook savory stews and vegetable dishes. Because the lid of the tagine traps steam and returns the condensed liquid to the pot, a minimal amount of water is needed to cook meats and vegetables to buttery tenderness. This cooking method is very practical in areas where water supplies are limited or where public water is not yet available; it also helps tenderize inexpensive cuts of meat.

Tagines often include various spices, such as turmeric, cinnamon, saffron, ginger, and cumin. Recipes can vary widely, from lamb to beef to chicken to fish; while some tagines feature dried fruit and nuts, you will also find fresh herbs, olives, preserved lemons, and even eggs and sausage. There is also a Berber tagine which distinguishes itself by how the vegetables are artistically arranged around the lamb for a beautiful presentation.

Moroccan Food for Good Health

Many of the ingredients found in Moroccan food promote good health, as Moroccan food tends to rely on whole food ingredients freshly prepared, using herbs and spices for flavor rather than deep frying.

Bread tends to be baked from whole grains, and many entrees include both vegetables and dried fruit to achieve that balance between sweet and savory that is characteristic of Moroccan food. **Here a few of the healthiest ingredients and dishes found in Moroccan cuisine:**

- *Chickpeas*

Also known as garbanzo beans or Bengal gram, chickpeas are a legume high in nutrients and highly digestible, a concern for some sensitive to beans. Chickpeas are rich in protein, fiber, folate, and many important dietary minerals like iron, phosphorous, and zinc. Chickpeas are found in many Moroccan dishes, including tagines, spreads to be served on bread, and a huge variety of soups and stews.

- *Turmeric*

The turmeric commonly used in cooking is a dried yellow-orange powder prepared from the rhizomes (root-like parts) of the turmeric plant, a member of the ginger family. Turmeric is used in many Asian dishes and is also commonly used in herbal medicine. Turmeric extracts have been shown to possess anti-fungal and anti-microbial properties and are under study for their potential effects on cancer, heart disease, diabetes, and other common diseases.

- *Ginger*

Ginger root is another medicinal rhizome used frequently in Moroccan cuisine. Medicinally, ginger is frequently used to treat mild nausea, though it is not recommended for pregnant women looking to treat morning sickness as it is an irritant. In the amounts typically used in cooking, ginger supplies a large amount of dietary manganese along with a bright warmth of flavor. Ginger is one of the most frequently used spices in Moroccan cuisine and is found in many dishes. It is often used in tagines and teas.

- *Whole Grains*

One of the most popular Moroccan foods across the globe is couscous. It is often served as a dish in Morocco, consisting of a bed of couscous served with a rich seven-vegetable sauce, sometimes topped with stewed meat and caramelized onions. This is a deeply traditional dish. Every family has its favorite blend of vegetables and spices. Traditional spices found in the recipe are turmeric, ginger, and pepper.

- *Whole Grain Bread*

Every culture has a starch component to their diet, and for Moroccans, the starches are primarily couscous and rolls baked from whole grains. These leavened whole-grain rolls accompany all of the vegetable dishes and meat stews. The traditional rolls are often spiced with fennel and anise seed for added flavor. Morocco also has a traditional sweet roll called the krachel, sweet bread flavored with anise, orange flower water, and sesame. These rolls are similar to brioche: the dough is rich and includes eggs and butter.

- *Vegetables*

Vegetables are a large component of the Moroccan diet. A vegetable medley salad precedes almost every meal. Commonly used vegetables include potatoes, tomatoes, peppers, artichokes, and carrots, among many others. Vegetables also round out most meat dishes, providing depth and flavor as well as nutrients and fiber. Of course, almost everywhere there are vegetables, chickpeas are present to add even more fiber and lots of protein.

- *Dried Fruit*

Dried fruit is often responsible for sweetening desserts. However, you will find dates, raisins, apricots, and prunes not only in sweets but also in savory dishes. One of the characteristics of Moroccan cuisine is the careful balance of sweet and savory in many recipes. Tagines are an excellent example. They are traditionally meat entrees where spiced meat is slow-cooked with vegetables and spices in a shallow baking dish with a tall, conical lid (the baking vessel is called a 'tagine').

Moroccan food is a very healthy national cuisine. With a heavy emphasis on vegetables, whole grains, and sweetening with fruit rather than refined sugar, this North African food tradition has served its followers well for centuries. The intriguing balance between sweet and savory in many dishes is not found in many other food traditions. Try a few Moroccan recipes in your kitchen, and enjoy the taste and reap the health benefits.

Why Moroccan Recipes Are So Popular?

If you have heard about Moroccan cuisine frequently, you wonder why this food is so popular. But is it worth the effort to try these exotic recipes?

There are many reasons why you should include Moroccan cuisine and Mediterranean recipes in your diet. **Some of the top reasons include:**

- **Moroccan food is based on healthy recipes.** These meals include a lot of vegetables with plenty of herbs and spices added in flavoring. Chicken and lamb are also frequently used in Moroccan cuisine. All these exotic recipes offer a delicious taste and fragrant aroma and the health benefits you will get. If you want to eat healthier but do not sacrifice taste and flavor, then Moroccan food is exactly what you're looking for.

- **Moroccan cuisine is extremely easy and simple to make.** You now have to spend hours preparing and cooking the ingredients, and the result is a well-balanced meal that is delicious and nutritious.

- **Moroccan cuisine offers versatility that many other foods do not.** The exotic recipes can be very versatile, and substitutions can be made if necessary. Moroccan food is influenced by North African culture, as well as Mediterranean recipes and flavors.

- **The Tagines used to put Moroccan food means that cooking time is very fast.** These clay cooking pots require less time; they are easy and simple to use and can make an attractive addition to any table. You can have a delicious dinner in a very short amount of time with Moroccan cuisine.

- **Weight loss will normally occur when you start eating Moroccan food.** Because Moroccan cuisine is based largely on vegetables and spices, it is considered a dieting plan that encourages weight loss and better health.

- **If you want a filling and delicious snack, then Moroccan cuisine fits the bill perfectly.** Combine some flatbread with various Moroccan olives and some different cheeses, and you will have a snack that you are proud to serve to guests who show up uninvited or that you are more than happy to eat yourself.

- **If you're looking for exotic recipes that Moroccan cuisine and foods fit in this category.** When you prepare Moroccan foods, it looks like you have spent a great deal of time and effort to create a delicious and exotic meal, but the truth is that the easy preparation and cooking with the Tagines made the meal a snap.

- **Many Moroccan foods are known to be soothing to the digestive system.** One of these is the Moroccan mint tea, which is delicious, both hot and cold, and can help soothe any digestive problems that you may have.

- **The biggest reason to try Moroccan cuisine is that these exotic recipes taste fabulous, and isn't that why you eat food in the first place?** After one taste, all of the other benefits of Moroccan food will be forgotten, and you will be hooked by flavor alone.

What Makes Cooking With Moroccan Tagines Special?

If you have never seen any Moroccan tagines before, you may be a bit surprised when you have a look at them. The first thought that normally comes to mind is what can you possibly cook with it? Or maybe you thought it would be stylish to serve your guests with this peculiar-looking pot? Anyway, **here are some reasons why cooking with these tagine cooking pots is special:**

- *An easy cooking experience*

Many people do not like to spend a lot of time cooking complicated dishes. Or maybe the main reason is that they do not want to waste whatever time they have in the kitchen preparing ingredients unless they happen to enjoy gourmet food. One of the things I like about Moroccan tagines is that cooking with them is easy. Anyone could do it. You don't need any other special kitchen equipment other than a stove. And you won't have to use different pots and pans for cooking one simple dish with it. It's so easy that here's a short rundown on how to cook with it, which anyone could try out.

- *Cook any type of stew*

Whether you prefer meat or vegetables, these tagine cooking pots are built to handle stews. Its cone-shaped lid ensures that the heat condenses at the top so that the dish does not dry up even if you leave it on the stove for a few hours. Just add some olive oil to the base of the pot, sear your meats to seal in the juices before removing them. Next, add all the spices and vegetables and stir them together before adding some water or broth along with the seared meat to cook until soft and tender. The base of the pot is deep enough, and depending on your serving size, you could choose either a small or large pot to cook your stew in.

- *Culturally rich and unique*

These lovely stews will taste fantastic with freshly baked bread, and you could even add in some nuts and apricots to make it tastier. It's a wonderful cultural dish that anyone could cook and is meant to be shared with family and friends. And the best part is that you don't even have to transfer the stew to another pot or bowl as you could just serve the stew from the tagine pot itself. Keeping the lid on it will keep the dish warm, and since the pot is made of clay, your stew won't cool off so fast. So you can be assured of a nice warm stew to enjoy with others.

. . .

So if you want to try something new, just get yourself a Moroccan tagine and have a wonderful time cooking the type of stews you will enjoy. Your family and friends will be flocking over to share the dish with you.

2

HOW DOES TAGINE WORK?

A TAGINE POT IS A CONE-SHAPED CLAY COOKING VESSEL FOR THE slowly simmered and generously spiced dishes of North Africa. It comes in a two-piece set, with a round and shallow base topped by a conical lid, tapering at the top with a knob that also serves as a handle to check on what's bubbling inside.

While tagines are similar to other thick-walled pots with tight-fitting lids, such as Dutch ovens, their conical shape makes them unique, promoting steam circulation with very little water. While the food is being cooked, the steam rises up into the cone, condensates, and falls back into the dish, continuously basting the other ingredients and keeping them moist and buttery. This was ingenious for nomads living in the desert, where water was scarce, and their shallow base's dual function for both cooking and serving food made them space-efficient, too. Tagines were used as portable ovens, placed over an open fire or a bed of coals.

Classic clay or earthenware tagines are usually unglazed, which lends the dishes they cook an earthy flavor. Still, you can find them nowadays in different types of materials, including glazed ceramics and a multitude of colors and designs.

What Are The Best Tagines To Buy?

Purists would insist that traditional unglazed clay or earthenware is the way to go. But if you're buying an authentic Moroccan clay tagine, do your homework. Health Canada has warned that some tagines may contain dangerous lead levels if the ceramic isn't glazed uniformly or the pottery isn't fired at a hot-enough temperature, so make sure you're getting one from a reputable manufacturer. Also, ensure that your tagine is meant for cooking rather than just for serving or decorative purposes. When cleaning an unglazed clay tagine, hot water and baking soda should suffice. If necessary, you can use a mild soap and rinse well. Remember that clay is very porous, so you don't want it to absorb a soapy taste.

Even without the traditional clay cooking vessel, you can still make a mean tagine—even in Morocco. In many authentic restaurants, the food may be brought to your table in an elegant tagine but not necessarily cooked in it. When you're cooking for a crowd, a plain old stainless-steel pot or Dutch oven might be the way to go.

You can find tagines made of different materials, such as

flameware (flameproof ceramic cookware), which can be used at a higher temperature than traditional clay tagines, or cast iron, such as Le Creuset, which some people may appreciate for its durability and the way it retains heat for longer. Cast iron is also way easier to take care of compared to clay. But no matter what kind of tagine you get, don't let it just sit pretty on your shelf. Put it to good use!

Are Tagines Healthy?

If you're a lover of Moroccan food, thinking about this cuisine probably brings to mind the delicious, slow-cooked, spicy meat dishes that are slowly and gently cooked in the magical tagine. Tagine refers to a conical-shaped dish used to cook food, and it is also used to refer to the food cooked in this dish as well.

The unique, conical shape of this dish results in a unique cooking environment that is both hot and moist. The base of the dish is shallow and wide, and the conical lid fits inside snugly. While the food is cooking, the steam rises up in the cone. Then, it condenses and begins to slide down the sides into the dish once again. Cooking with a tagine is much like cooking with a Dutch oven or a crockpot.

Since the tagine is both a cooking dish and a serving dish that will keep your food warm, cooking in this vessel is different. The cooking process is great for making healthy, delicious foods. Like in a slow cooker, the food in a tagine is boiled or steamed instead of fried. Meats and veggies are often used in a tagine, combined with a bit of olive oil and favorite seasonings, and then the food is left to cook for hours uninterrupted. Dishes that have lamb or beef in them may take 4-5 hours of simmering, while chicken dishes may only take 2-3 hours. When you cook in a tagine, you'll get food that is packed with flavor, and you'll usually end up with a thick, tasty sauce as well.

If you enjoy slow cooking food and going with healthy dishes, you're sure to enjoy cooking in a tagine. You'll get the delicious, slow-cooked flavor with the unique twist that clayware adds to all your favorite dishes.

Can You Cook a Tagine in the Oven?

Although they were traditionally cooked on an open fire, today, tagines are most commonly used on the stovetop with a diffuser. However, a newer tagine pot may be ovenproof, so you are free to experiment and see which kind of cooking you like best!

When cooking a tagine (dish) on the stovetop, it's important to remember that the tagine cookware can't come into direct contact with the stovetop; a diffuser must be placed between them.

What Do You Cook in a Tagine?

A tagine is both the cookware and the dish that is cooked in it. Tagine food, otherwise known as Maghrebi, is a slow-cooked stew made with meat, poultry, fish, or vegetables with spices, fruit, and nuts. A small hole at the top of the cookware's lid periodically releases some steam to ensure that the food does not get too soggy.

Tagines are normally shared dishes served with lots of flatbread; the tagine vessel will sit in the middle of the table, and families or groups will gather around, using fresh bread to spoon up the ingredients. Eating in this way brings a great social element to mealtimes!

Tagine recipes are the most popular dishes made in these types of cookware, but that certainly doesn't restrict this cooking device. You can use all sorts of different ingredients to make each tagine unique - think of your ideal combination of vegetables, meat, fish, and pulses, and go from there! With so many different combinations, you could make a different one each week and not get bored.

However, tagines can also be used for other slow-cooked

meals. Use this ceramic to make Shakshuka, a breakfast dish eaten widely across the Middle East and North Africa. It consists of eggs in a delicious tomato sauce and is mopped up with lots of bread. You could even move away from African food and use your tagine to make a delicious Indian curry or a European-style stew. The possibilities are endless!

How Do You Cook in a Tagine?

Tagine cooking can seem daunting, but it's very easy to create delicious one-pot meals with these gorgeous pieces of cookware. If you wonder how to cook with a tagine, read on as we'll go through it all!

The most important part of learning how to use a tagine is knowing the importance of seasoning. Depending on the material used in the tagine, there is a good chance that it will need to seasoned periodically throughout its life. This is especially the case for cast iron cookware. Cast iron is generally much more durable and long-lasting when properly cared for. Seasoning strengthens and seals the cast iron and adds a non-stick layer so that you never have to worry about your food sticking to your tagine.

To season a tagine, follow these simple steps. It's not complicated, but the process does take some time, so it's best to do it when you are at home for several hours.

Seasoning a cast iron tagine:

- Ensure that the tagine is fully dry, and using a paper towel or cooking brush, coat the tagine with vegetable oil all over (inside and outside).
- Put the tagine into a cold oven and then turn the temperature on to 300°F.
- Leave the tagine in the oven for two hours.
- Turn the oven off and leave the tagine in there, waiting

until it is completely cool before you remove it.
- Wash the tagine and brush it with olive oil before its first use.

Once your tagine is seasoned, you are ready to cook!

While tagine recipes can vary greatly, **here are some simple steps to bear in mind every time you make a Moroccan tagine:**

- Create a base layer - tagines nearly always have a base of onions, celery, or carrots with garlic. The base layer serves to make a bed for other ingredients, so they don't stick to the bottom.
- Add a layer of olive oil.
- Arrange the main ingredient - whether that be lamb, chicken, fish, vegetables, or tofu - to the center of the base layer. Then put any extra vegetables around the main ingredient.
- Season all of the ingredients - add spices, like cinnamon, turmeric, cilantro, or cumin, to all of the ingredients that are in the tagine so far.
- Add garnishings and more vegetables - you might want to layer your vegetables and create a conical shape, mimicking the shape of the tagine. You'll also want to add garnishes, like herbs or more flavorful fruits and vegetables. Apricots are the traditional fruit served with tagines, but be creative! Tagines aren't stirred during cooking, so make sure that your dish looks how you want it to at this stage.
- Add your liquid; this is normally water, stock, or broth.
- Remember to use a diffuser when cooking on the stovetop.
- Let it simmer on low heat for the required amount of

time -this largely depends on what food you are cooking.

How to Clean a Tagine

Once you've finished your tagine cooking, you're going to want to know how to clean it properly.

Once your tagine cookware is cool, warm water and baking soda is generally sufficient to hand-wash a tagine. When it is clean, it should be fully dried and brushed with olive oil before storing. When storing, don't put the lid on fully - this gives better circulation of air.

You can use salt or steel wool for any stubborn remains of a tagine stuck to the bottom.

What is the Benefit of Cooking in a Tagine?

Tagines are the perfect piece of equipment for fantastic one-pot cooking. One-pot cooking is great for many reasons. It reduces the amount of washing up, but food cooked in this way can be extra succulent and tasty because of it!

Slow cooking has amazing benefits. It gives the spices and flavors time to absorb into the meat or vegetable components of the dish, giving it a rich taste that is often missing in quickly cooked dishes. However, it's difficult to slow cook without the right tools; many dishes will dry out easily if cooked in a standard pot or a pan.

This is where tagine cooking excels. The style of the pot, with the solid ceramic base and conical lid, is great for retaining and locking in moisture. Vegetables and meat have moisture within themselves, normally reduced by steam coming out during the cooking process.

However, tagines trap that moisture; it is sealed in and

circulated thanks to the shape of the lid. Food will never dry out in this Moroccan cooking dish, so meals can be slow-cooked for hours, where they can develop a more intense flavor over time, and the components of the meal will be gloriously tender. Using a Moroccan tagine pot is a fantastic way to upgrade your cooking.

3

HOW TO USE A TAGINE

Follow this step-by-step guide to using a tagine:

- **Season the tagine.** A tagine should be seasoned before using to strengthen and seal it and, if it is unglazed, to remove the taste of raw clay. To season, soak the lid and base in water for 2 hours. Dry the tagine and brush the interior and exterior of the lid and base with olive oil. Place the cookware in a cold oven and set the oven to 300°F. Bake for two hours, then turn off the oven and let tagine completely cool inside. Wash the tagine and brush once more with olive oil before using it.
- **Make the base layer.** The first step of cooking tagine is to place a layer of vegetables across the base of the pot, creating a cushion for the remaining ingredients. A bed of chopped onions, celery, or carrots will keep the meat from sticking to the bottom and burning during cooking. Chopped or whole garlic cloves can be added to the base for flavor.

- **Add olive oil.** Adding enough olive oil is important to make a rich sauce in the tagine; most recipes recommend at least ¼ cup.
- **Add meat, poultry, or fish.** In the center, add meat, poultry, or fish. Arrange in a mound in the center, leaving enough room to add other vegetables around the edges. Arrange vegetables around the meat.
- **Season with spices.** Sprinkle spices generously over the meat and vegetables to make a rich, flavorful sauce. Spices that work well in tagine recipes are cardamom, clove, cinnamon, ground coriander, cumin, paprika, mace, nutmeg, peppercorn, ground ginger, and ground turmeric.
- **Garnish the dish.** Presentation is an important part of making a tagine. You can add color with strips of bell peppers, olives, or preserved lemon. Add tied bundles of fresh herbs like parsley, oregano, or cilantro.
- **Add enough water or broth.** Adding liquid such as water or chicken broth to the tagine keeps food moist while cooking. Pour water or chicken stock carefully into the side of the tagine, around 1 ½ cups for a small tagine, and 2 ½ cups for a large tagine. Adjust as needed according to the recipe.
- **Cook the tagine.** Avoid high heat to keep the tagine from cracking. Place it above the heat source, not directly on it (a diffuser is needed for electric stovetops). Place over low to medium-low heat until it reaches a slow simmer. The cooking time for recipes can vary, with fish and chicken being shorter and beef and lamb taking longer.
- **Check the liquid.** After 2 hours, check the level of the

cooking liquid. If the liquid has already thickened, add another ¼ cup of liquid.
- **Serving the tagine.** Tagines double as a beautiful serving dish. Make sure to allow the tagine to cool down for 15 minutes before serving. Traditionally, tagine is served as a dish to share communally, using Moroccan bread to scoop and up the meat, vegetables, and sauce. Tagine is also delicious served over couscous.

Using a Tagine at Home

When cooking with a tagine, there are a few things you need to plan for, from preparing the vessel to having the correct equipment for your stovetop. Before using a tagine for the first time, you'll want to season it. This includes soaking it, rubbing with oil, and placing it in the oven for a couple of hours. The process removes any raw clay taste (if it is unglazed) and strengthens the material.

The traditional cooking method with a tagine is to place the vessel over large bricks of charcoal purchased specifically for their ability to stay hot for hours. You can try cooking a tagine over charcoal (be sure to leave adequate space between the coals and the tagine, or the temperature inside the vessel will be too high), but it may be more practical to use your tagine in a low oven or on the stovetop, using the lowest heat necessary to keep the stew simmering gently. Because the bottom of the tagine should not come in direct contact with its heat source, a diffuser—a circular piece of aluminum placed between the tagine and burner—is required if not cooking over a gas flame or charcoal.

Cooking Tagines That Will Help You Manage Your Time

If you plan to have guests over to your home, you may be pressured to cook up a storm to impress them. If you would like to have a relaxing meal without stressing out cooking tons of different dishes, you may want to consider getting some cooking tagines.

Why Use Moroccan Tagines?

People who cook with Moroccan tagines will tell you that they are used for cooking excellent stews. Whether you prefer any meat or vegetarian stew, cooking tagines are ideal because they are made of clay, and cooking with them will help soften the meat and vegetables, making the dish tastier. On top of that, the shape of these cooking tagines will help prevent the stew from drying up since the cone-shaped top helps condense the steam. So you could leave the dish to cook for hours without worrying that you'll end up with a burnt dish later on.

Is The Cooking Process Long?

Cooking any stew with these Moroccan tagines will help free up your time to do other things. All you need to do is to prepare the pretty easy ingredients. Depending on whether you like your stew spicy or non-spicy, get the meats and vegetables ready. Pour some olive oil at the base of the tagine and sear the meats. This helps to seal in the juices. Remove the meats and add in your chopped garlic, onions, and spices. Cook them for a few minutes before adding in your other chopped vegetables. Stir everything well before adding in the broth or plain water. Season with salt and pepper before adding in the meats. Cover the dish and allow to simmer for a few hours or until the meat is tender enough to your liking.

Time To Do Other Things

While the stew is simmering away, you could use that time to do other things. Perhaps you would like to cook another dish or prepare a simple salad and dessert? Whipping up a simple salad will not take up much of your time. Panicking over what to prepare for desert? Just get some ice cream which everyone will love. You could also buy some freshly baked bread to go with your wonderful stew. Once you're done setting up the table and preparing everything else, your stew will be ready. Leave it to cool for a while before serving some to your guests.

Talk about saving time. Cooking with Moroccan tagines will allow you to allocate your time to get other things ready for your relaxing dinner. And your guests will enjoy the meal.

How to Use Cooking Tagines to Whip Up Delicious Holiday Dishes

The holidays are just around the corner. Many folks are looking forward to heading back home for a wonderful Thanksgiving meal with their families and friends. Why not make this Thanksgiving a bit more special by using cooking tagines to whip up some delicious stews other than the normal turkey? **Here are a few suggestions that you could try out:**

- *Delicious lamb stew*

Imagine a delicious lamb stew where the meat is practically falling off the bone tenderly as you scoop it out of the pot. Talk about having a really good meal with family and friends. This dish is easy to prepare as you do not have to worry about it being complicated. It is really easy to cook with Moroccan tagines as you can sear the meat on the pot first to seal in the juices. Cook the rest of the vegetables and spice before adding the meat back into the cooking tagine to simmer and boil for a few hours. By the time you get ready to serve the dish, your family members and friends would all be there waiting to have an enjoyable meal with you. Complement the traditional turkey with this delicious lamb stew if you happen to have a big family gathering. This will be a wonderful meal to enjoy together.

- *An alternative to salads*

If you are bored with the typical salad greens, you could cook up a wonderful vegetarian stew with these Moroccan tagines. It will also be ideal if you happen to have any vegetarians coming over to your home for the meal. The thing about cooking tagines is that all you need to do is add in oil, heat it up, and stir fry the spices with the different types of vegetables together before adding water to simmer and thicken. If you are worried that the entire dish will dry up, that's where the cone-shaped lid comes in handy as it helps to condense the heat keeping the dish from drying up.

- *Leftovers are not wasted*

Not if you are wondering what to do with all the leftover meat and vegetables from your wonderful Thanksgiving meal, you could put them all together to create a delicious stew that everyone can enjoy. No point wasting any of the food. It's about being as creative as can be with how you prepare the food. The stew will taste great with freshly baked bread and lovely tea.

Everyone loves the holiday season. Not only do you get to shop, but the thought of getting back together with family and friends to enjoy delicious meals is worth looking forward to. Have a wonderful time with your family and friends.

4

WHAT BEGINNER CHEFS NEED TO APPRECIATE CONCERNING COOKING WITH TAGINE

HOME CHEFS ARE OFTEN SEARCHING FOR NEW COOKING METHODS OR approaches to enhance their food, and one such technique that people might perhaps not even have tested is tagine cooking. Tagine cooking has been around for hundreds of years. Tagine cuisines are given their names for the earthenware pot, typically a flat circular plate covered by a large domed cover that remains on the plate in the cooking process, which originates from North Africa and is typically associated with Moroccan cuisine.

Tagines usually come in two varieties: cooking and serving, with both of them being the same thing save because the serving ones are commonly glazed and colorfully decorated. The nomadic Berber of Morocco used the early tagines, and tagine cooking was habitually carried out over charcoal with the most common ingredients containing lamb, poultry, and fish. The tagine became favored because it needs a very tiny bit of water, a rare material in that part of the world. Also, with this cooking technique, you can surely cook ingredients for hours with the domed top covered for circulating water vapor inside the dish to keep the food wet while also saturating the food with oil and seasonings.

Fortunately for our modern cooks, tagines can easily be discovered in almost every common store that provides cookware, such as Williams Sonoma. The tagines have a collection of dimensions and designs to satisfy everybody, and the price tag is constantly set at around $20 up to hundreds of dollars. Budget and personal preference will likely be the biggest considerations in deciding on your first tagine, but keep in mind when doing so, practically all of the glazed tagines are produced for serving but not indeed for tagine cooking.

. . .

Before you go into the fundamentals of tagine cooking, it's a fantastic idea to get your tagine ready first so that you could be able to obtain ideal results. Submerge your tagine in water for a couple of hours; after that, coat the base and the cover interior with some olive oil, then place it in an unheated oven before increasing the heat to 350 degrees Fahrenheit. After 2 hours, remove the tagine and allow it to cool. You might then repeat the olive oil process before storing it.

A brief online search can reveal thousands of different recipes for you to try, with many of them relying on conventional lamb and chicken ingredients. The fun part of tagine cooking is that you can easily experiment with different vegetables and herbs, aiming to provide your many alternatives with distinctive flavors every time. The actual cooking time can be anywhere from 45 mins to a few hours, so be sure to refer to each instruction for the exact cooking time, especially if cooking for visitors, and no matter how rushed, make sure that you never set your tagine over high heat as this can most likely crack and damage the dish. With appropriate care of your pot, you can be cooking fantastic brand-new meals for years to come.

Recipe Ideas for Your Moroccan Tagine

Now that you've mastered how to use your tagine, **here are some creative recipe ideas using your tagine:**

- **Moroccan lamb tagine.** Tender seasoned lamb stew

meat with chickpeas, dates, oranges, and almonds is a classic sweet and savory Moroccan dish. Serve over couscous to soak up its delicious sauce.

- **Moroccan chicken with preserved lemons and olives.** A fragrant chicken stew with spiced bone-in chicken thighs or chicken breasts cooked with tangy preserved lemons, sauteed onions, and savory green olives. Finish with sprigs of fresh cilantro.

- Moroccan chicken and apricot. The secret to this dish is using the North African spice blend, Ras El Hanout, made with cardamom, clove, ground cinnamon, coriander, ground cumin, paprika, mace, nutmeg, peppercorn, and turmeric. The spice blend adds a bold flavor to the chicken and makes a rich sauce. Dried apricots, tomatoes, and honey are added to the dish for a combination of savory and sweet.

- **Kefta Mkaouara (Moroccan meatballs).** A Moroccan meatball dish in a zesty tomato sauce. Eggs are often added to the dish at the end of cooking, resulting in poached eggs perfect for dipping with crusty Moroccan bread.

- **Mqualli (Fish tagine).** A classic fish dish with potatoes, tomatoes, and bell peppers. Any firm fish can be used, such as swordfish, sea bass, or dorado. The sauce base is typically made with ginger, saffron, and extra virgin olive oil.

- **Moroccan vegetable tagine.** A vegetarian-friendly tagine made with chickpeas, carrots, russet potatoes, and sweet potatoes and seasoned with harissa paste and a touch of sweetness from honey and golden raisins.

- **Shakshuka.** Shakshuka is a simple and delicious dish of eggs poached in a spiced tomato sauce cooked with onions, chili peppers and garnished with herbs. Shakshuka is traditionally cooked in a tagine, but it can also be made in a cast-iron pan or skillet.

Ideas On What to Cook With a Tagine Pot

If you have just received a tagine pot as a gift from friends and you happen to be someone who loves to cook, you will enjoy the dishes and stew that this pot can whip up. **Here are 3 ideas on what you can cook with the tagine pot:**

- *Meat Tagines*

When we talk about Moroccan tagines, the first thought to whiz past your mind would be the delicious meat tagines prepared with it. Normally, it would be a lamb dish or stew as tagines are great for cooking meats till they are tender. The thickness of the stew would depend on how you like it. Since everyone has their taste, and if you happen to be cooking it, you get to decide on how spicy or thick you would like it to be. Then again, some may not like a lamb. So don't worry as you could always cook using other meats of your choice like chicken, fish or even pork. As long as the people you are serving the food to can consume the meats, then you are good to go as you wouldn't want to offend anyone.

- *Vegetable Tagines*

Those who are vegetarian or vegan will not have any problem cooking with Moroccan tagines as they could whip up tasty vegetable tagines independently. If you plan to have guests over, you could have a combination of a meat tagine and vegetable tagine to serve them. If you think that these vegetable dishes are boring, I can assure you that they will be a blast if you follow the Moroccan recipes. Best eaten with freshly baked bread or couscous. If you want to improvise, you could eat them with rice as well.

- *Sweet Tagines*

If you would like to be a bit more adventurous, you could try cooking some sweet tagines. These are used as celebratory dishes.

Well, there's always something to celebrate in life. Anyway, these sweet tagines could be meat or vegetables, but they will be sweet because of the many different types of dried fruits and nuts added to them. You could add dried apricots, prunes, raisins, dates, apples, pears, red currants, along with the usual spices and ground black pepper to the dish. Your guests will enjoy it if they would like to try something new.

So cooking with a tagine pot is quite fun as there is a variety of food to whip up. There are different flavors and tastes to try out.

5
HOW TO PREPARE THE TOP HEALTHY DELICIOUS MOROCCAN TAGINE RECIPES

FOOD IN MOROCCO PLAYS AN IMPORTANT ROLE IN TRADITIONAL LIFE. From weddings to baptisms to circumcisions, it is the basis of social gatherings and celebrations. From couscous to tagines and pastilles, the delicate flavors are a blend of tastes of many civilizations. Arab, Berber, Middle Eastern, French and Jewish are just some of the influences on what is today recognized as Moroccan cuisine.

Over the centuries, the chefs of the royal kitchens refined the cuisine to create mouth-watering local dishes to titillate our taste buds. Apricots, dates, figs, and raisins local foods, while almonds, pine nuts, and pistachios are used extensively. Spices such as cinnamon, cumin, turmeric, ginger, saffron, and mint lend an exotic flavor. And mint tea is the favorite drink, with freshly squeezed juices a close second.

A truly traditional Moroccan dish is a tagine, a stew of vegetables with poultry or beef and dried fruit. The fruit is added towards the end to give an overall sweetness to the dish. The vegetables are set around the meat, placed in the center of the pot, and the fruit. The tagine is then covered and cooked slowly over a charcoal stove (called kanoun). Tagines also contain salted or preserved lemons, giving them a unique flavor that can't be replicated using fresh lemons. Traditionally, the tagine is served with couscous, rice, or bread. When eating, start on the outside with the vegetables, working your way to the meat at the heart of the dish.

Here are the top healthy and delicious Moroccan Tagine recipes to get you started

---

Moroccan Tagine

Tagines are Moroccan slow-cooked meat, fruit, and vegetable dishes that are almost invariably made with mutton. Using lamb cuts down the cooking time, but if you can find good hogget (older than lamb, younger than mutton, commonly labeled 'baking legs' and sold cheaply), that will do very well

---

Prep time: 15 mins

Servings: 5 servings

Ingredients

- 1 tablespoon olive oil
- 2 large onions, peeled and sliced into rings
- 2 pounds lamb meat, cut into 1 1/2-inch cubes
- 1 teaspoon ground cumin
- 1 teaspoon ground coriander seed
- 1 teaspoon ground ginger
- 1 teaspoon ground cinnamon
- salt to taste
- 1 teaspoon ground black pepper
- 4 pears - peeled, cored, and cut into 1 1/2 inch chunks
- ½ cup golden raisins
- ½ cup blanched slivered almonds

Directions

- Step 1

Heat the oil in a large pot or Dutch oven over medium heat. Fry the onion in the oil until soft. Add the lamb meat to the pan, and fry until just browned on the outside. Season with cumin, coriander, ginger, cinnamon, salt, and pepper. Pour just enough water into the pot to cover the meat. Cover, and simmer over low heat for 1 1/2 to 2 hours until meat is tender and the mixture is stew-like. Displace lid a little after an hour if there appears to be too much liquid.

- **Step 2**

Add the pears, golden raisins, and almonds to the stew, and cook for another 5 minutes or so until the pears are soft. Serve with rice.

Nutrition Facts

394 calories; protein 26.4g; carbohydrates 42.7g; fat 14.5g; cholesterol 71.3mg; sodium 68.3mg

Moroccan Fish Tagine

This delicious healthy dish common to North Africa, particularly Morocco, is one of my favorites when entertaining guests. The wonderful spices blended with fresh vegetables and fish is a crowd-pleaser. The fish is marinated in a chermoula sauce to soak up all the wonderful spices before cooking. This dish is prepared in a traditional method in a ceramic tagine but can be prepared in a heavy-lidded pot. This dish, as it cooks, emits some of the most wonderful smells throughout the house. Serve with couscous or rice and crusty bread to mop up all the wonderful sauce!

Prep time: *50 mins*
Servings: *6 servings*

∾

Ingredients

Chermoula Marinade:

- ½ cup olive oil
- ½ cup chopped fresh cilantro
- ½ cup chopped fresh parsley
- ½ lemon, juiced
- 6 cloves garlic, minced
- 1 teaspoon ground paprika
- ½ teaspoon ground ginger
- ½ teaspoon ground cumin
- ½ teaspoon salt
- ¼ teaspoon ground saffron (Optional)

Fish Tagine:

- 1 ½ pounds cod fillets, cut into bite-sized pieces
- 1 tablespoon olive oil
- 1 large onion, cut into rings
- 1 large carrot, peeled and cut into matchsticks
- 2 potatoes, peeled and sliced 1/4-inch thick

- 1 large green bell pepper, sliced into rings
- 3 tomatoes, seeded and cut into strips
- ¼ cup chopped fresh cilantro

Directions

- Step 1

Mix 1/2 cup olive oil, 1/2 cup cilantro, parsley, lemon juice, garlic, paprika, ginger, cumin, salt, and saffron in a large glass or ceramic bowl. Add cod and mix well. Cover and marinate in the refrigerator for 2 hours.

- Step 2

Heat 1 tablespoon olive oil in a large pot or tagine. Layer onion rings, carrot matchsticks, and potato slices in the pot in that order. Remove cod from marinade and spread evenly over potatoes. Cover cod with green bell pepper rings and tomato strips. Sprinkle 1/4 cup cilantro on top. Pour marinade over cilantro.

- Step 3

Cover pot tightly and cook over low heat until potatoes are tender and cod flakes easily with a fork, about 1 hour.

Nutrition Facts

---

368 calories; protein 23.1g; carbohydrates 22g; fat 21.4g; cholesterol 40.9mg; sodium 289.4mg

Moroccan Chicken Tagine with Preserved Lemons, Fennel, Olives, and Harissa

Prep time: 30 mins
Servings: 4 servings

∼

Ingredients

- 1 teaspoon ground paprika
- 1 teaspoon ground cumin
- 1 teaspoon salt
- ½ teaspoon ground cayenne
- ½ teaspoon ground cinnamon
- ½ teaspoon ground turmeric
- ground black pepper
- 4 (6 ounces) bone-in chicken thighs, skin removed

- 2 tablespoons olive oil
- 1 fennel bulb, trimmed and thinly sliced
- 1 large red onion, thinly sliced
- 3 cloves garlic, minced, or more to taste
- 1 (15 ounces) of can garbanzo beans, drained, divided
- 1 cup chicken broth
- 1 cup pitted green olives, divided
- 3 tablespoons harissa, or to taste
- ½ preserved lemon, thinly sliced, divided
- 1 teaspoon grated ginger root (Optional)
- 5 cherry tomatoes, halved, or more to taste
- ¼ cup toasted almonds

Directions

- **Step 1**

Mix paprika, cumin, salt, cayenne, cinnamon, turmeric, and black pepper together in a small bowl.

- **Step 2**

Pat chicken thighs dry and place them in a resealable plastic bag. Sprinkle paprika mixture over chicken thighs; massage the bag to coat chicken evenly.

- **Step 3**

Heat oil in a tagine over medium heat. Add chicken; cook until browned, 2 to 4 minutes per side. Transfer to a plate. Cook and stir fennel, onion, and garlic in the tagine. Stir in half of the garbanzo beans, chicken broth, 1/2 cup green olives, harissa, 1/2 of the preserved lemon, and ginger.

- **Step 4**

Lay chicken over garbanzo bean mixture; sprinkle remaining olives on top. Scatter cherry tomatoes on top. Cover and simmer over medium-low heat until chicken is tender, 45 minutes to 1 hour.

- **Step 5**

Combine remaining garbanzo beans with 2 tablespoons of broth from the tagine in a food processor or blender; blend into a thin paste.

- **Step 6**

Transfer chicken to a serving dish. Stir garbanzo bean paste into the tagine. Simmer until flavors combine, about 5 minutes. Spoon broth mixture over chicken.

- **Step 7**

Garnish with remaining preserved lemon and toasted almonds.

Nutrition Facts

517 calories; protein 36g; carbohydrates 31.4g; fat 28.5g; cholesterol 102.4mg; sodium 3350.6mg

Stovetop Moroccan Tagine

An exotic warm stew that is loved by all and is very easy to make. Also delicious as a vegetarian dish, without chicken. Serve over couscous.

Prep time: 15 mins
Servings: 6 servings

Ingredients

- 1 tablespoon olive oil
- 2 skinless, boneless chicken breast halves - cut into chunks
- ½ onion, chopped
- 3 cloves garlic, minced
- 1 small butternut squash, peeled and chopped
- 1 (15.5 ounces) can garbanzo beans, drained and rinsed
- 1 carrot, peeled and chopped
- 1 (14.5 ounces) can diced tomatoes with juice
- 1 (14 ounces) of can vegetable broth
- 1 tablespoon sugar
- 1 tablespoon lemon juice
- 1 teaspoon salt
- 1 teaspoon ground coriander
- 1 dash cayenne pepper

Directions

- Step 1

Heat the olive oil in a large skillet over medium heat, and cook the chicken, onion, and garlic for about 15 minutes, until browned.

- Step 2

Mix the squash, garbanzo beans, carrot, tomatoes with juice, broth, sugar, and lemon juice into the skillet. Season with salt, coriander, and cayenne pepper. Bring the mixture to a boil, and continue cooking for 30 minutes until vegetables are tender.

Nutrition Facts

---

266 calories; protein 14.1g; carbohydrates 44.7g; fat 4.3g; cholesterol 20.3mg; sodium 878.5mg

---

Instant Pot Moroccan Chicken Tagine

Your Instant Pot replaces the traditional clay or ceramic cone-shaped cooking pot used in Moroccan cuisine (the tagine). The word 'tagine' also refers to the slow-cooked, stew-like dish that is prepared in it. This chicken tagine features the authentic flavors of preserved lemons and olives, with a delicious combination of spices typically used in Moroccan cooking.

Prep time: 25 mins

Servings: 6 servings

∽

Ingredients

- 2 tablespoons minced fresh garlic
- 1 ¼ teaspoons paprika
- ¾ teaspoon ground ginger
- ¾ teaspoon ground turmeric
- ⅛ teaspoon saffron powder
- 1 ½ pound skinless, boneless chicken breasts, cut into bite-sized pieces
- 1 preserved lemon
- 2 tablespoons extra-virgin olive oil
- 2 tablespoons butter
- 2 medium red onions, sliced
- 1 cinnamon stick
- 1 cup pitted and halved Mediterranean olives
- 1 cup chicken broth
- 1 tablespoon chopped fresh flat-leaf parsley
- 1 tablespoon chopped fresh cilantro

Directions

- **Step 1**

Combine garlic, paprika, ginger, turmeric, and saffron in a large bowl. Add chicken pieces and mix until coated with spices. Cover and refrigerate, 3 to 4 hours or overnight.

- **Step 2**

Cut the preserved lemon into quarters. Remove pulp from the peel and remove seeds from the pulp. Mince pulp and set aside. Cut lemon peel into strips and set aside.

- **Step 3**

Turn on a multi-functional pressure cooker (such as Instant Pot®) and select Saute function. Heat olive oil and butter in the cooker; add chicken. Cook chicken until browned, about 3 minutes per side. Transfer chicken to a plate, reserving drippings in the pot.

- **Step 4**

Place onions and lemon pulp into the hot pot and cook, occasionally stirring, until onions have softened, about 5 minutes. Add cinnamon stick, place chicken on top, and scatter olives and lemon peel over the chicken. Pour in chicken broth. Close and lock the lid. Select high pressure according to manufacturer's instructions; set timer for 10 minutes. Allow 10 to 15 minutes for pressure to build.

- **Step 5**

Release pressure using the natural-release method according to manufacturer's instructions, about 10 minutes. Unlock and remove the lid carefully, turning it away from you. Transfer contents to a large serving bowl. Sprinkle with parsley and cilantro and serve immediately.

Nutrition Fact

257 calories; protein 24.6g; carbohydrates 8.7g; fat 13.8g; cholesterol 75.8mg; sodium 2538.4mg.

Moroccan Chicken Tagine

Sweet and savory stewed chicken with dried fruits and exotic spices. Serve this on top of couscous and top with toasted almonds and fresh cilantro. Children love the familiarity of the 'sweet' spices and dried fruits.

Prep time: 20 mins
Servings: 6 servings

Ingredients

- ¼ cup ground cinnamon
- ¼ cup ground cumin
- 2 tablespoons ground turmeric
- 2 tablespoons ground coriander
- 2 tablespoons ground ginger
- 2 tablespoons crushed dried mint
- 1 tablespoon salt
- 2 teaspoons ground black pepper
- ½ cup chopped dried apricots
- ¼ cup raisins
- ¼ cup olive oil, or as needed
- 4 bone-in chicken thighs
- ½ small onion, minced
- 2 teaspoons chopped garlic
- 1 cup chicken broth
- ¼ cup honey
- ½ bunch fresh cilantro, chopped
- ¼ cup toasted sliced almonds

Directions

- Step 1

Mix cinnamon, cumin, turmeric, coriander, ginger, mint, salt, and pepper together in a bowl. Measure out 1/2 cup spice mix and set the remaining aside for another use.

- Step 2

Bring a small pot of water to a boil; add apricots and raisins.

Cook until fruit is soft, about 5 minutes. Drain, reserving 1/2 cup of the cooking water.

- **Step 3**

Pour enough olive oil into a large skillet or Dutch oven to coat the bottom; turn heat to medium. Coat chicken with the 1/2 cup spice mix and place in the hot oil; cook until golden brown and release easily from the skillet, 3 to 4 minutes per side.

- **Step 4**

Mix onion and garlic into the skillet with chicken; cook and stir until fragrant, 2 to 3 minutes. Add apricots; raisins reserved 1/2 cup water from fruit, chicken broth, and honey; reduce heat to low and cover. Cook until chicken is very tender, 1 1/2 to 2 hours.

- **Step 5**

Serve chicken garnished with cilantro and almonds.

Nutrition Facts

371 calories; protein 15.4g; carbohydrates 35.8g; fat 20.4g; cholesterol 43.5mg; sodium 1375.1mg

Moroccan Turkey Tagine Stew

A classic Moroccan tagine stew with warm spices, vegetables, and dried fruit adds leftover turkey for a twist on a traditional dish.

Prep time: 35 mins
Servings: 8 servings

~

Ingredients

- 2 tablespoons olive oil
- ¾ cup chopped red onion
- 2 cups thinly sliced carrots
- 2 cups thinly sliced parsnips
- 2 teaspoons finely chopped garlic
- 1 tablespoon ras el hanout seasoning

- 1 (15 ounces) of can garbanzo beans, drained, rinsed
- 1 (14.5 ounces) of can Hunt's Diced Tomatoes, undrained
- 1 (14 ounces) of can chicken broth
- ½ cup water
- ½ cup chopped dried apricots
- ⅓ cup chopped pitted prunes or whole raisins
- 3 cups shredded cooked turkey
- ¼ cup chopped fresh cilantro
- Greek yogurt and hot cooked couscous, optional

Directions

- **Step 1**

Heat oil in a Dutch oven or large saucepan over medium-high heat. Add onion; cook 3 minutes or until tender, stirring occasionally. Add carrots and parsnips; cook 5 minutes or until crisp-tender. Stir in garlic and ras el hanout seasoning; cook 1 minute or until fragrant.

- **Step 2**

Stir in beans, undrained tomatoes, broth, water, apricots, and prunes. Bring to a boil. Reduce heat and simmer 30 minutes or until vegetables are tender, stirring occasionally.

- **Step 3**

Stir in turkey; heat 5 minutes more or until hot. Top each serving with cilantro. If desired, top with yogurt and serve with couscous on the side.

Notes

For homemade ras el hanout seasoning, stir together 1/2 teaspoon cumin, 1/2 teaspoon ginger, 1/2 teaspoon turmeric, 1/4 teaspoon black pepper, 1/4 teaspoon white pepper, 1/4 teaspoon ground coriander, 1/4 teaspoon ground red pepper, 1/4 teaspoon ground allspice, 1/4 teaspoon ground nutmeg and 1/8 teaspoon cinnamon in a small bowl. Use as directed in the recipe. Shredded rotisserie chicken can be used in place of turkey.

Nutrition Facts

257 calories; protein 19.3g; carbohydrates 30.9g; fat 6.9g; cholesterol 41.1mg; sodium 565.4mg

Moroccan Ksra

This simple Moroccan Ksra (or Kesra) features semolina and aniseed and is ideal for a Moroccan Tagine meal.

Prep time: *2 hrs*

Servings: *16 servings*

Ingredients

- ⅞ cup water
- 2 ¼ cups bread flour
- ¾ cup semolina flour
- 1 teaspoon anise seed
- 1 ½ teaspoons salt
- ½ teaspoon white sugar
- 2 teaspoons active dry yeast
- 1 tablespoon olive oil
- 1 tablespoon sesame seeds (Optional)

Directions

- **Step 1**

Place the first set of ingredients in the pan of the bread machine in the order recommended by the manufacturer. Select DOUGH cycle; press Start. Do not put the olive oil or sesame seeds in.

- **Step 2**

When the dough cycle signals its end, remove the dough from the machine, and punch down. Divide the dough into two halves, and shape it into balls. Flatten the balls to a 3/4 inch thickness. Place them on a lightly floured baking sheet. Cover with towels, and let rise until double in size for about 30 minutes.

- **Step 3**

Preheat the oven to 400 degrees F (200 degrees C). Brush the top of each loaf with olive oil, and sprinkle with sesame seeds if you like. Prick the tops of the loaves all over using a fork.

- **Step 4**

Bake for 20 to 25 minutes in the preheated oven or until the loaves are golden and sound hollow when tapped. Serve warm or cool.

Nutrition Facts

83 calories; protein 2.6g; carbohydrates 14.5g; fat 1.5g; sodium 219.1mg

Moroccan Chicken Tagine with Caramelized Pears

Chicken cooked in a tagine is always meltingly tender. Adding sweet, caramelized pears at the end makes this Moroccan dish irresistible.

Prep time: 20 mins
Servings: 6 servings

Ingredients

- 7 tablespoons olive oil, divided
- 2 onions, peeled and sliced
- 1 whole chicken, cut into pieces
- 1 teaspoon ground turmeric
- 1 teaspoon ground cumin
- 1 teaspoon ground coriander
- 1 teaspoon salt
- 3 cinnamon sticks
- 2 bay leaves, crushed

- 1 bunch fresh cilantro, chopped
- 2 tablespoons fresh ginger root, peeled and minced
- ½ cup water
- 2 tablespoons butter
- 2 pears, cored and sliced
- 2 tablespoons honey

Directions

- **Step 1**

Preheat oven to 350 degrees F (175 degrees C).

- **Step 2**

Heat 2 tablespoon olive oil in a skillet over medium heat and cook onions until softened and browned, 8 to 10 minutes. Transfer onions into a tagine. Layer chicken pieces on top of onions.

- **Step 3**

Combine turmeric, cumin, ground coriander, and salt in a small bowl; mix well with the remaining 5 tablespoons olive oil. Spread spice mixture onto the chicken pieces. Add cinnamon pieces, bay leaves, ginger, and cilantro. Pour in 1/2 cup of water and cover tagine with a lid.

- **Step 4**

Bake in the preheated oven until chicken is no longer pink at the bone and the juices run clear for about 50 minutes. An instant-read thermometer inserted near the bone should read 165 degrees F (74 degrees C).

- **Step 5**

Melt butter in a skillet over low heat while the chicken is cooking. Add sliced pears and honey and cook, while stirring, until the honey has caramelized.

- **Step 6**

Remove tagine from the oven and stir in caramelized pears. Return to the oven and cook for an additional 10 minutes.

Note

Use a heavy-bottomed ceramic or cast iron casserole if you don't have a tagine.

Nutrition Facts

---

533 calories; protein 32.6g; carbohydrates 19.8g; fat 36g; cholesterol 109.8mg; sodium 508.7mg

---

Moroccan Carrots

Want a nice side dish and don't want to heat up the kitchen? Great dinner idea for those hot summer nights.

Prep time: 15 mins
Servings: 4 servings

Ingredients

- 4 large carrots, peeled and grated
- 1 (16 ounces) of can garbanzo beans (chickpeas), drained and rinsed
- ½ cup raisins
- 2 tablespoons olive oil
- 1 tablespoon lemon juice
- ½ teaspoon cumin

- ½ teaspoon chili powder
- salt and ground pepper to taste
- ¼ cup crumbled feta cheese

Directions

- Step 1

Combine carrots, garbanzo beans, and raisins together in a bowl.

- Step 2

Whisk olive oil, lemon juice, cumin, chili powder, salt, and ground black pepper together; stir into carrot mixture. Marinate carrot mixture for 2 hours. Serve with crumbled feta cheese.

Nutrition Facts

307 calories; protein 8.3g; carbohydrates 47.9g; fat 10.4g; cholesterol 8.3mg; sodium 538.2mg

Instant Pot Chicken Tagine with Butternut Squash and Spinach

Butternut squash, chicken thighs, spinach, and spices are thrown together and cooked quickly and easily in an Instant Pot in this Moroccan-inspired chicken tagine.

Prep time: 15 mins
　Servings: 6 servings

~

Ingredients

- 4 tablespoons extra-virgin olive oil, divided
- 3 ½ teaspoons kosher salt, divided
- 2 teaspoons ground cinnamon
- 2 teaspoons ground cumin
- 2 teaspoons sweet paprika

- 1 teaspoon ground coriander
- ½ teaspoon ground black pepper
- 1 ½ pound skinless, boneless chicken thighs, trimmed and cut into 1 1/2-inch piece
- 1 large yellow onion, thinly sliced lengthwise
- 4 cloves garlic, smashed
- 4 teaspoons finely grated fresh ginger
- 2 ½ cups water
- 2 cups peeled and cubed (3/4-inch) butternut squash
- 1 (14.5 ounces) of can diced tomatoes in juice
- 1 (5 ounces) package baby spinach leaves
- 3 tablespoons lemon juice
- 2 teaspoons lemon zest
- salt and ground black pepper to taste

Directions

- Step 1

Stir 2 tablespoons oil, 2 1/2 teaspoons kosher salt, cinnamon, cumin, paprika, coriander, and 1/2 teaspoon black pepper together in a small bowl to form a paste. Toss 1 tablespoon paste with chicken in a medium bowl.

- Step 2

Turn on a multi-functional pressure cooker (such as Instant Pot®) and select Saute function. Heat remaining oil until shimmering, about 1 minute. Add onion and 1 teaspoon kosher salt; cook, occasionally stirring, until softened, about 6 minutes.

- Step 3

Stir in remaining spice paste, garlic, and ginger. Cook, constantly stirring, until fragrant, 30 seconds to 1 minute. Stir in water, scraping up any browned bits from the bottom using a wooden spoon. Add butternut squash, tomatoes with their juices, and chicken; stir to combine, then distribute the mixture evenly. Close and lock the lid and move the pressure valve to seal. Select high pressure according to manufacturer's instructions; set timer for 3 minutes. Allow 10 to 15 minutes for pressure to build.

- Step 4

Release pressure using the natural-release method according to the manufacturer's instructions for 10 minutes. Release remaining pressure carefully using the quick-release method according to the manufacturer's instructions, about 5 minutes. Unlock and remove the lid.

- Step 5

Stir spinach into the pot and cover without locking the lid into place. Let stand until spinach wilts, about 3 minutes. Stir in lemon juice and zest; taste, and season with salt and pepper.

Nutrition Facts

---

296 calories; protein 21.5g; carbohydrates 13.1g; fat 17.4g; cholesterol 70mg; sodium 1343.3mg

---

Instant Pot Lamb Tagine with Lentils

This lovely Moroccan-inspired Instant Pot tagine has a wonderful taste and a little kick. The spices combine to present a warm flavor, and the honey and raisins soften the tangy tomatoes with a bit of sweetness. You can double the spices if you like, but start with listed measurements and adjust per your tastes! Serve with rice.

Prep time: *10 mins*
Servings: *6 servings*

Ingredients

- 2 tablespoons ghee (clarified butter)
- 1 onion
- 1 pound cubed lamb stew meat

- 2 large tomatoes, diced
- 1 ½ cups diced potatoes
- 2 cloves garlic, minced
- 1 teaspoon salt (Optional)
- ½ teaspoon ground black pepper
- ½ teaspoon ground cumin
- ½ teaspoon ground coriander
- ½ teaspoon ground turmeric
- ½ teaspoon ground cinnamon
- ½ teaspoon ground ginger
- ½ teaspoon paprika
- 1 teaspoon chili flakes
- 2 tablespoons tomato paste
- 2 cups chicken broth
- 1 cup dry lentils
- ⅓ cup raisins, or more to taste
- 2 tablespoons honey
- 1 pinch salt and ground black pepper to taste (Optional)

Directions

- Step 1

Turn on a multi-functional pressure cooker (such as Instant Pot) and select Saute function. Add ghee. Add onions and cubed lamb to the melted ghee; cook and stir until lamb is browned and onion is soft and translucent, 5 to 7 minutes. Stir in tomatoes, potatoes, and garlic. Cook for 2 more minutes.

- Step 2

Mix in salt, pepper, cumin, coriander, turmeric, cinnamon,

ginger, paprika, and chili flakes. Stir in tomato paste. Add chicken broth, lentils, raisins, and honey; stir until all ingredients are well combined.

- **Step 3**

Turn Saute mode off. Close and lock the lid. Set vent to 'Sealing' and select Meat/Stew mode according to manufacturer's instructions; set timer for 30 minutes. Allow 10 to 15 minutes for pressure to build.

- **Step 4**

Release pressure using the natural-release method according to manufacturer's instructions, for 10 minutes. Turn vent and release remaining pressure carefully using the quick-release method according to the manufacturer's instructions. Season with salt and pepper, if needed.

Nutrition Facts

401 calories; protein 22.3g; carbohydrates 46.7g; fat 14.6g; cholesterol 56.3mg; sodium 849.2mg

Moroccan Sardine Meatballs

High in omega-3s, these are a healthier alternative to regular meatballs!

Prep time: 10 mins
　　Servings: 2 servings

∼

Ingredients

- 1 (4 ounces) of can sardines, drained
- 2 eggs
- 2 tablespoons dry bread crumbs
- ½ teaspoon ground paprika
- ½ teaspoon ground turmeric
- ½ teaspoon ground ginger
- ½ teaspoon garlic powder
- ½ teaspoon onion powder
- salt and ground black pepper to taste
- 2 tablespoons olive oil

- ¼ onion, chopped
- 2 cloves garlic, chopped
- 1 (14.5 ounces) of can canned diced tomatoes
- 2 tablespoons ground coriander
- ½ teaspoon ground cumin

Directions

- Step 1

Place sardines in a food processor; puree until smooth. Add eggs, bread crumbs, paprika, turmeric, ginger, garlic powder, onion powder, salt, and black pepper. Pulse briefly until well-combined. Shape mixture into small balls.

- Step 2

Heat oil in a large skillet over medium heat. Add onion and garlic; cook and stir until fragrant, about 5 minutes. Stir in tomatoes, coriander, and cumin. Reduce heat, cover, and simmer sauce until flavors combine for about 15 minutes. Stir in meatballs and simmer until heated for about 5 minutes.

Nutrition Facts

418 calories; protein 24.3g; carbohydrates 21g; fat 27g; cholesterol 266.5mg; sodium 777.6mg

Moroccan Kofte and Sausage Stew

A North African casserole ideal for a small party. Just adjust the ingredients to your liking.

Prep time: 20 mins
Servings: 8 servings

~

Ingredients

Harissa:

- 10 dried red chile peppers
- 4 tablespoons olive oil, divided
- 3 cloves garlic, minced
- ½ teaspoon sea salt
- 1 teaspoon ground coriander
- 1 teaspoon ground caraway seeds
- ½ teaspoon ground cumin

Stew:

- 1 bunch fresh cilantro, or to taste
- 1 ⅓ pounds ground beef
- 1 onion, finely chopped
- 1 fresh red chile pepper, finely chopped
- 1 teaspoon ground cumin
- 1 teaspoon ground cloves
- 1 egg
- ½ teaspoon sea salt
- 1 tablespoon olive oil
- 1 (16 ounces) of can diced tomatoes
- 1 (14.5 ounces) of can chicken stock
- ¼ teaspoon ground cinnamon
- 3 links Merguez sausage, cut into pieces

Directions

- **Step 1**

Soak dried chile peppers in hot water for 30 minutes. Drain. Remove stems and seeds.

- **Step 2**

Blend chiles with 2 tablespoons of olive oil, garlic, and 1/2 teaspoon salt in a food processor. Add coriander, caraway seeds, and cumin; blend to form a smooth paste. Transfer to an airtight container. Drizzle about 2 tablespoons olive oil on top to keep fresh.

- **Step 3**

Chop 1/2 of the cilantro and stem the rest. Combine chopped

cilantro with beef, onion, cilantro, fresh chile, cumin, and cloves. Add egg and sea salt; mix to combine. Form into about 26 small meatballs, each about the size of a walnut.

- Step 4

Heat olive oil in a large frying pan. Fry meatballs in batches until browned all over, about 5 minutes. Remove meatballs and add 2 tablespoons harissa to the pan; cook, stirring, for 1 minute. Add tomatoes, chicken stock, and cinnamon. Simmer for 15 minutes.

- Step 5

Return meatballs to the pan and stir in sausage. Simmer until sausage is heated through and no longer pink in the center, about 20 minutes. Stir in remaining cilantro.

Notes

Store harissa in an airtight container and keep for a month in the refrigerator.
Use any good-quality sausage you like.

Nutrition Facts

345 calories; protein 20.1g; carbohydrates 9.6g; fat 25.1g; cholesterol 90mg; sodium 534mg

Moroccan Chickpea Stew with Quinoa

This Moroccan chickpea stew is super flavorful, warm, hearty, easy to make, cheap, and to top it off, really good for you. Give it a try!

Prep time: 25 mins
Servings: 6 servings

Ingredients

- 1-pint cherry tomatoes
- 3 tablespoons olive oil, or to taste, divided
- 1 pinch salt and ground black pepper to taste
- 1 onion, diced
- 3 cloves garlic, minced, or more to taste
- 1 ½ teaspoon of smoked paprika
- 1 ½ teaspoon of ground cumin

- ¾ teaspoon ground coriander
- ⅛ teaspoon cayenne pepper (Optional)
- 1 teaspoon salt, or to taste
- ground black pepper, or to taste
- 1 (15.5 ounces) of can diced tomatoes
- 1 (4.5 ounces) of can chopped green chiles
- 1 (15.5 ounces) of can chickpeas, drained and rinsed
- 3 cups of water
- 1 ½ cups of uncooked quinoa
- 2 tablespoons of plain Greek yogurt
- 1 tablespoon of hummus spread
- 1 tablespoon of water
- ¼ teaspoon white vinegar
- 2 green onions, sliced (Optional)
- ¼ cup chopped fresh cilantro, or to taste

Directions

- Step 1

Preheat the oven to 425 degrees F (220 degrees C). Line a baking sheet with aluminum foil.

- Step 2

Spread cherry tomatoes on the prepared baking sheet. Drizzle with 1 tablespoon olive oil. Sprinkle salt and pepper over tomatoes and toss to coat evenly.

- Step 3

Roast in the preheated oven until the tomatoes blister and pop and skins start to char, 15 to 20 minutes.

- **Step 4**

Meanwhile, heat the remaining olive oil in a large Dutch oven over medium-high heat. Add onion and cook until translucent, 4 to 5 minutes. Add garlic, paprika, cumin, coriander, cayenne pepper, salt, and pepper. Cook until fragrant, 30 to 60 seconds. Add tomatoes and green chiles; bring to a boil. Reduce stew to a simmer and add chickpeas. Add the cherry tomatoes and their juices. Cover and simmer for 30 minutes.

- **Step 5**

While the stew simmers, bring 3 cups of water and quinoa to a boil in a saucepan. Reduce heat to medium-low, cover, and simmer until quinoa is tender, 15 to 20 minutes.

- **Step 6**

Mix Greek yogurt, hummus, 1 tablespoon water, and vinegar together to make the sauce. Season with salt and pepper.

- **Step 7**

Serve the stew over quinoa. Top with the yogurt sauce, green onions, and cilantro.

Note

Substitute rice for the quinoa if desired.

Nutrition Facts

359 calories; protein 11.9g; carbohydrates 53.6g; fat 11.3g; cholesterol 0.9mg; sodium 1022.4mg

Moroccan Vegetable Stew with Couscous

This hearty vegetarian stew combines great fall/winter vegetables with a spicy Moroccan flair. Stands alone as a complete meal.

Prep time: 30 mins
Servings: 6 servings

Ingredients

- 4 teaspoons extra-virgin olive oil, divided
- 1 cup chopped onion
- 1 cup sliced leek, 1/2-inch-thick
- 1 clove garlic, minced
- ½ teaspoon ground coriander
- ⅛ teaspoon ground cumin
- ⅛ teaspoon cayenne pepper
- 6 cups vegetable broth
- 2 cups cubed peeled butternut squash in 1/2-inch pieces
- 1 (15.5 ounces) of can chickpeas, drained and rinsed
- 1 ½ cups peeled and cubed Yukon Gold potatoes
- 1 cup peeled and cubed turnips
- 1 cup carrot slices, 1/2-inch thick
- 1 tablespoon of harissa
- 1 ½ teaspoon of tomato paste
- ¾ teaspoon of salt
- 1 ¼ cups of water
- 1 (6 ounces) package quick-cook couscous mix (such as Near East Mediterranean Curry)
- ¼ cup of chopped fresh flat-leaf parsley
- 1 ½ teaspoon of honey
- 1 lemon, cut into wedges

Directions

- **Step 1**

Heat 2 teaspoons of oil in a large saucepan over medium-high heat. Add onion and leek; saute until translucent, about 5 minutes. Add garlic, coriander, cumin, and cayenne pepper; cook, constantly stirring, for 1 minute.

- **Step 2**

Pour in vegetable broth. Stir in butternut squash, chickpeas, potatoes, turnips, carrots, harissa, tomato paste, and salt. Bring to a boil. Cover, reduce heat and simmer for 30 minutes.

- **Step 3**

Bring water, couscous spice packet, and remaining olive oil to a boil in a separate saucepan. Stir in couscous. Cover and remove from heat. Let stand until couscous is tender, about 5 minutes.

- **Step 4**

Add parsley and honey to the stew. Place 1/2 cup couscous into each serving bowl and top with 1 cup stew. Squeeze a lemon wedge into each dish.

Notes

Omit the honey for a vegan option.
Substitute parsnips for turnips, if desired.

Nutrition Facts

341 calories; protein 11.2g; carbohydrates 66.5g; fat 5.4g; sodium 1371mg

---

Moroccan-Spiced Chicken Skewers

Prep time: 45 mins

Servings: 4 servings

~

Ingredients

- ¼ cup extra-virgin olive oil
- ¼ cup chopped fresh mint leaves
- ¼ cup chopped fresh cilantro
- 2 tablespoons fresh lemon juice
- 2 teaspoons honey

- 1 ½ teaspoon of kosher salt
- 2 cloves garlic, minced
- 1 teaspoon paprika
- 1 teaspoon ground cumin
- ½ teaspoon ground coriander
- ½ teaspoon ground cinnamon
- ¼ teaspoon ground cayenne pepper
- 4 (6 ounces) of skinless, boneless chicken breast halves, cut into 1 1/2 inch cubes

Sauce:

- 2 cups whole-milk Greek yogurt
- ½ cup fresh lemon juice
- ¼ cup finely chopped mint leaves
- 2 cloves garlic, minced
- 1 teaspoon finely grated fresh lemon zest
- 1 teaspoon kosher salt
- 2 green bell peppers, cut into cubes
- 1 small red onion, cut into 8 wedges
- bamboo skewers, soaked in water for 30 minutes

Directions

- Step 1

Whisk olive oil, 1/4 cup mint, cilantro, 2 tablespoons lemon juice, honey, 1 1/2 teaspoon salt, 2 cloves garlic, paprika, cumin, coriander, cinnamon, and cayenne in a large bowl. Reserve 1/4 cup marinade in a separate bowl.

- Step 2

Place chicken in a large resealable plastic bag. Pour marinade over chicken. Press air out of the bag and seal tightly. Turn the bag to distribute the marinade. Place in a bowl and refrigerate for 5 hours.

- **Step 3**

Whisk yogurt, 1/2 cup lemon juice, 1/4 cup mint, 2 cloves garlic, lemon zest, and 1 teaspoon salt together in a bowl to make the sauce. Cover and place in the refrigerator.

- **Step 4**

Toss green bell peppers and red onion in the reserved 1/4 cup marinade. Remove chicken from the bag and discard all marinade. Thread chicken, peppers, and onion alternately onto skewers.

- **Step 5**

Preheat an outdoor grill for medium-high heat and lightly oil the grate. Arrange skewers on the grill. Close lid and cook, turning once or twice until chicken is firm to the touch, 8 to 10 minutes. Remove from grill and let stand for 2 to 3 minutes. Serve with cold sauce.

Note

Nutrition data for this recipe includes the full amount of marinade ingredients. The actual amount of marinade consumed will vary.

Nutrition Facts

496 calories; protein 42.8g; carbohydrates 17.1g; fat 28.5g; cholesterol 119.4mg; sodium 1355.5mg.

Moroccan Harira (Bean Soup)

A (mostly) vegetarian, a shoestring-budget meal that will leave you feeling both very satisfied and with tons of leftovers. Bonus: it's super-healthy and easy to prepare.

Prep time: 15 mins
Servings: 10 servings

Ingredients

- 6 cups beef stock
- 1 cup dry lentils
- 1 tablespoon olive oil, or to taste
- 1 onion, chopped
- 1 cinnamon stick
- 1 teaspoon minced fresh ginger root
- 1 teaspoon ground turmeric
- 1 teaspoon ground cumin
- 1 teaspoon ground black pepper
- 1 (15 ounces) of can garbanzo beans, drained
- 1 (15 ounces) of can red kidney beans, rinsed and drained
- 1 (14 ounces) of can diced tomatoes
- 1 cup cooked quinoa (Optional)
- 1 bunch flat-leaf parsley leaves and thinner stems, chopped
- 1 bunch cilantro leaves and thinner stems, chopped
- 1 lemon, or to taste, juiced

Directions

- **Step 1**

Stir beef stock and lentils together in a large pot; bring to a boil, reduce heat to low, and keep at a simmer while preparing onion.

- **Step 2**

Heat olive oil in a skillet over medium heat. Cook and stir onion, cinnamon stick, ginger, turmeric, cumin, and black pepper in the hot oil until the onion is translucent for about 5 minutes; add to stock mixture.

- **Step 3**

Pour garbanzo beans, kidney beans, tomatoes, and quinoa into the stock mixture; stir and bring mixture to a boil. Stir parsley and cilantro into the stock mixture; reduce heat to low and cook mixture at a simmer until the lentils are tender, about 45 minutes. Drizzle lemon juice over the soup before serving.

Notes

To make the soup wholly vegetarian, trade out the beef stock for vegetable stock.

If you do use quinoa, be sure to prepare it separately from the soup (1/2 cup unprepared = 1 cup prepared). Throwing it into the soup unprepared will cause it to absorb all the liquid, and you will be left with a very, very thick stew.

Nutrition Facts

---

261 calories; protein 14.4g; carbohydrates 42g; fat 3.9g; sodium 298.5mg

---

Moroccan Fig Pork Roast

A succulent, savory, and sweet pork roast, ideally served over vegetable rice or couscous.

Prep time: 10 mins
Servings: 8 servings

Ingredients

- 1 (5 pounds) of boneless pork loin roast
- 1 tablespoon curry powder
- 1 tablespoon ground turmeric
- 1 tablespoon garam masala
- 2 teaspoons ground ginger
- 2 teaspoons chili powder
- 1 teaspoon ground cumin
- 1 pinch ground cayenne pepper
- salt and ground black pepper to taste
- 2 tablespoons olive oil

- 2 tablespoons butter
- 3 cloves garlic, roughly chopped
- 1 onion, roughly chopped
- 2 tablespoons fig compote
- 1 (14.5 ounces) of can whole peeled tomatoes
- 1 cup chicken broth

Directions

- **Step 1**

Preheat an oven to 350 degrees F (175 degrees C). Pat pork roast dry with a clean towel. Mix curry powder, turmeric, garam masala, ground ginger, chili powder, cumin, cayenne, salt, and pepper in a small bowl. Rub spice mixture all over the pork roast.

- **Step 2**

Heat the olive oil and butter in a large, heavy-bottom pot or Dutch oven over medium-high heat. Place the seasoned pork roast into the pot and cook until evenly browned, about 2 minutes on each side. Remove pork and set aside. Stir in the garlic and onion; cook and stir until the onion has softened and turned translucent for about 5 minutes. Stir in the fig compote until well blended. Return pork to the pot, coating it with the fig mixture. Pour in the tomatoes and chicken broth. Cover, and bring to a boil.

- **Step 3**

Place covered pot in the preheated oven. Cook until the pork is no longer pink in the center, about 2 hours. An instant-read thermometer inserted into the center should read 145 degrees F (63 degrees C).

Nutrition Facts

488 calories; protein 46.9g; carbohydrates 6.1g; fat 29.8g; cholesterol 142.7mg; sodium 304.5mg

Moroccan Chickpea Stew

This recipe came to be as a way to use the kale that was flourishing in the garden. It could also incorporate other vegetables - whatever is in your fridge that needs to be used. Serve over couscous.

Prep time: 15 mins
Servings: 4 servings

Ingredients

- 1 tablespoon olive oil
- 1 small onion, chopped
- 2 cloves garlic, minced
- 2 teaspoons ground cumin
- 2 teaspoons ground coriander
- ½ teaspoon cayenne pepper, or to taste
- 1 teaspoon garam masala
- ½ teaspoon curry powder
- 1 pinch salt
- 3 potatoes, cut into 1/2-inch cubes
- 1 (14.5 ounces) of can diced tomatoes, undrained
- 1 cup tomato sauce
- 1 cup golden raisins
- water, or enough to cover
- 1 (14.5 ounces) of can chickpeas, drained and rinsed
- 1 bunch kale, ribs removed, chopped
- ½ cup chopped fresh cilantro

Directions

- Step 1

Heat the olive oil in a large pot over medium heat; cook the onion and garlic in the hot oil until the onions are translucent, 5 to 7 minutes. Stir the cumin, coriander, cayenne pepper, garam masala, curry powder, and salt into the onion and garlic; cook together until fragrant, about 1 minute. Add the potatoes, diced tomatoes, tomato sauce, and raisins to the pot. Pour enough water over the mixture to cover; bring to a simmer and cook until the potatoes are soft, 10 to 15 minutes.

- **Step 2**

Add the chickpeas and kale to the pot; simmer until the kale wilts, about 3 minutes. Sprinkle the cilantro over the stew and immediately remove the pot from the heat.

Nutrition Facts

476 calories; protein 15.7g; carbohydrates 96.1g; fat 6.5g; sodium 1263.3mg

Savory Quail Tagine

Quail cooked in savory spices with vegetables in a tagine for a change from the usual. If you do not own a tagine, a Dutch oven will work perfectly well.

Prep time: 20 mins
Servings: 2 servings

Ingredients

- 1 whole quail
- 2 tablespoons ras el hanout
- 2 tablespoons olive oil, or more as needed
- 3 ounces carrots, cut into 1-inch rounds
- 1-ounce leeks, cut into 1/2-inch rounds
- 1 clove garlic, peeled and crushed
- 10 dried apricots
- 8 ounces potatoes, cut into 1-inch slices
- 5 cherry tomatoes
- 1 teaspoon loomi Aswad (dried black lime seasoning)
- 2 tablespoons chopped fresh cilantro

Directions

- Step 1

Rub the ras el hanout onto the entire surface of the quail, including beneath the wings and legs. Use all the seasoning. Allow it to rest at room temperature for 30 minutes.

- Step 2

Preheat oven to 375 degrees F (190 degrees C). Remove the middle rack(s) and place the lower rack in its lowest position.

- Step 3

Place a diffuser over the stove burner, so the tagine base is not in direct contact with it. Place the tagine base on the diffuser and heat over medium heat; add the oil. When oil is hot, add the carrots and leeks. Saute until leeks are tender, about 5 minutes. Separate the leeks into single rounds using a wooden spoon. Push the vegetables to the sides of the tagine and add the quail and garlic. Cook the quail on all sides until nicely browned, about 10 minutes. You may need to add a bit of oil occasionally, depending on the bird's fat content. Remove tagine from heat.

- **Step 4**

Arrange apricots, potatoes, and tomatoes around the edges, leaving the quail uncovered. Sprinkle all ingredients with the loomi Aswad.

- **Step 5**

Cover the tagine place in preheated oven. Roast until the internal temperature of the quail has reached 150 degrees F, 35 to 40 minutes.

- **Step 6**

Uncover the tagine and, if desired, brown quail under the broiler for 2 to 3 minutes.

- **Step 7**

Sprinkle with fresh coriander before serving. Serve with ice-cold milk.

Notes

Tagines are perfect for cooking because you don't need to use much liquid. The cone-shaped top allows all condensation to drip back into the base created a succulent, natural sauce. Therefore, the lid must stay on the tagine the entire cooking time. Opening the tagine while cooking will allow the steam to escape and result in dry or even burned food.

Nutrition Facts

493 calories; protein 16.7g; carbohydrates 64.6g; fat 21.6g; cholesterol 41.4mg; sodium 81.1mg

Moroccan-Spiced Pork Roast

Serving a gorgeous, fancy-looking holiday roast doesn't have to be complicated, time-consuming, or expensive. This pork loin

proves exactly that. This is fast, easy, and affordable, but it looks like a million dollars when you bring it to the table. The beautifully warming and aromatic spices really work so well with a pork roast - I hope you give it a try soon!

Prep time: *30 mins*

Servings: *12 servings*

∽

Ingredients

- 1 (3 pounds) boneless pork loin roast
- 5 teaspoons kosher salt
- 2 tablespoons olive oil

For the Moroccan Spice Rub:

- 2 teaspoons ground cumin
- 1 teaspoon ground coriander
- 1 teaspoon ground ginger
- 1 teaspoon freshly ground black pepper
- 1 teaspoon smoked paprika
- ¼ teaspoon cayenne pepper
- ½ teaspoon ground cinnamon
- ¼ teaspoon ground cloves
- ¼ teaspoon ground allspice
- 3 tablespoons honey, or as needed
- 8 baby potatoes
- 2 carrots, cut into 2-inch chunks

- 2 Anaheim chile peppers, halved and seeded
- 1 red onion, roughly chopped
- 2 tablespoons olive oil
- salt to taste

For the Yogurt Sauce (Optional):

- ½ cup plain Greek yogurt
- 2 tablespoons thinly sliced fresh mint
- 1 clove garlic, finely crushed

Directions

- **Step 1**

Butterfly the pork loin by cutting almost all the way through, starting on the thinnest side, keeping your knife flat and parallel to the cutting board. Stop about 1 inch from the opposite edge you started so that the meat opens up like a book. A few more shallow cuts can be made if the pork is not opening up enough to flatten out, but do not cut all the way through; otherwise, you'll end up with two pieces.

- **Step 2**

Season the butterflied pork on both sides with kosher salt and let sit out at room temperature for 30 to 45 minutes, or 2 to 3 hours in the fridge.

- **Step 3**

Preheat the oven to 350 degrees F (175 degrees C). Grease a

roasting pan with 2 tablespoons olive oil. Pat the tenderloin dry with a paper towel.

- **Step 4**

Mix cumin, coriander, ginger, black pepper, smoked paprika, cayenne, cinnamon, cloves, allspice, and honey together in a bowl with a spoon. Spread about half of the spice mixture inside the butterflied pork, fold it back together, and spread the remaining mixture all over the surface. Use 3 or 4 pieces of kitchen string to tie the loin up every few inches, cutting off the extra string.

- **Step 5**

Toss potatoes, carrots, chile peppers, and onion with olive oil and salt in a bowl.

- **Step 6**

Place the pork into the prepared roasting pan and surround it with a vegetable mixture.

- **Step 7**

Roast in the preheated oven until an instant-read thermometer inserted into the thickest part of the loin reads at least 140 to 145 degrees F (60 to 63 degrees C), about 1 hour and 15 minutes. Remove from the oven and turn roast over with tongs in pan drippings. Transfer to a plate, cover loosely with foil and let rest for 15 minutes.

- **Step 8**

Increase oven temperature to 425 degrees F. Toss vegetable mixture in pan drippings and return to the oven to crisp up, about 10 minutes.

- **Step 9**

Combine yogurt, mint, and garlic in a small bowl for sauce.

- **Step 10**

Remove strings on the roast. Slice, spoon pan drippings over and serve with vegetables and yogurt sauce.

Notes

You can use any size pork loin roast.

Patting the pork roast dry before applying the Moroccan spice rub will make it easier to spread.

Roasting the vegetables while the pork loin rests is only necessary if they need further cooking.

Nutrition Facts

333 calories; protein 23.2g; carbohydrates 32.9g; fat 12.2g; cholesterol 56.4mg; sodium 876.6mg

Moroccan Chicken Thighs

Quick and easy thighs with complex Moroccan flavors. Serve with rice, garnished with lemon wedges.

Prep time: 10 mins
Servings: 4 servings

Ingredients

- 8 bone-in chicken thighs
- kosher salt and ground black pepper to taste
- 1 ½ cups chicken broth
- 3 tablespoons paprika
- 3 tablespoons ground cumin
- 3 teaspoons minced fresh ginger root
- 3 teaspoons ground turmeric

- 2 teaspoons ground cinnamon
- 1 lemon, zested and juiced
- olive oil, or to taste
- 1 tablespoon canola oil, or to taste
- ½ white onion, chopped
- 1 cup pimento-stuffed green olives
- 2 tablespoons chopped fresh parsley

Directions

- Step 1

Season chicken thighs with salt and pepper. Let come to room temperature, about 30 minutes.

- Step 2

Preheat the oven to 375 degrees F (190 degrees C).

- Step 3

Combine chicken broth, paprika, cumin, ginger, turmeric, cinnamon, and 2 teaspoons lemon zest in a bowl.

- Step 4

Heat oils in a cast-iron skillet until they begin to smoke. Add chicken thighs, skin-side down, and cook for 4 minutes. Flip thighs and continue cooking until skin is crispy, about 4 minutes more. Transfer to a plate. Saute onion in the skillet until softened, 3 to 5 minutes. Pour chicken broth mixture carefully over onion; scrape up any browned bits off the bottom of the skillet.

- **Step 5**

Return chicken thighs to the skillet. Spoon some of the liquid over the thighs.

- **Step 6**

Transfer skillet to the preheated oven; bake until chicken thighs are no longer pink in the center, 25 to 30 minutes.

- **Step 7**

Add olives to the skillet. Drizzle lemon juice over the thighs and garnish the whole dish with parsley.

Note

Substitute 1 tablespoon onion powder for the fresh onion, if desired. Add to the chicken broth mixture.

Nutrition Facts

539 calories; protein 39.2g; carbohydrates 14.3g; fat 37.7g; cholesterol 130.6mg; sodium 1815mg.

Chicken Tagine with Couscous

This Moroccan-inspired chicken tagine with couscous recipe is a great meal that can be made in just 20 minutes. It's the perfect option for a midweek supper that the whole family can enjoy! This mouth-watering tagine is so easy to make at home. Each chicken breast is cooked in a rich tomato-based sauce. The warming sauce is infused with Moroccan spices with a hint of garlic and ginger. This chicken tagine is just bursting with flavor. Leftovers can be stored in an airtight container in the fridge for up to 2 days. Reheat thoroughly before serving again. This dish can be served with rice, new potatoes, or simply on its own with a chunk of crusty bread for dipping in the tomato sauce. Delicious!

Prep time: 20 mins
Servings: 6 servings

Ingredients

- 1 ¾ pound skinless, boneless chicken breast halves - cut into 1-inch pieces
- 2 large onions, thinly sliced
- ½ cup coarsely chopped dried apricots
- ⅓ cup raisins
- 1 ¼ cups low-sodium chicken broth
- 2 tablespoons tomato paste
- 2 tablespoons lemon juice
- 2 tablespoons all-purpose flour
- 1 ½ teaspoons ground ginger
- 1 ½ teaspoon ground cumin
- 1 teaspoon ground cinnamon
- ½ teaspoon black pepper
- ¼ teaspoon curry powder (Optional)
- ⅛ teaspoon cayenne pepper (Optional)
- 1 cup couscous
- 1 cup boiling water

Directions

- **Step 1**

Place the chicken, onions, apricots, and raisins into a slow cooker. In a bowl, whisk together the chicken broth, tomato paste, lemon juice, flour, ginger, cumin, cinnamon, black pepper, curry powder, and cayenne. Pour the mixture over the chicken in the cooker. Cover, set the cooker to High, cook 2 1/2 hours, or set the cooker to Low and cook for 5 hours.

- **Step 2**

Place the couscous into a saucepan, stir in the boiling water, cover, and let stand until the water is absorbed and the couscous is tender for about 5 minutes. Fluff the pasta with a fork. Scoop onto plates, and serve with chicken tagine.

Nutrition Facts

341 calories; protein 32g; carbohydrates 45.7g; fat 3.3g; cholesterol 69.1mg; sodium 131.5mg.

Moroccan Potato Bean Soup

A delicious, creamy soup and enjoyed anytime. The soup is medium spicy. If you favor a less spicy soup, reduce the amount of peppers used. Vegetable stock may be used instead of water.

Prep time: 15 mins
Servings: 8 servings

∽

Ingredients

- 6 cups water
- 1 (15 ounces) of can kidney beans
- 3 tablespoons olive oil
- 2 onions, chopped
- 2 potatoes, peeled and cubed
- 3 tablespoons chicken bouillon powder
- ½ teaspoon ground turmeric
- ½ teaspoon ground black pepper
- ½ teaspoon ground white pepper
- ½ teaspoon cayenne pepper (Optional)
- 2 teaspoons curry powder
- 2 tablespoons soy sauce
- ½ cup whole milk
- ½ cup half-and-half
- ½ cup dry potato flakes
- ¼ cup chopped green onions

Directions

- Step 1

In a medium-size cooking pot, add water and white kidney beans and bring to boil. Reduce heat and simmer for 15 minutes.

- Step 2

In a frying pan, saute onions in olive oil until lightly brown.

- Step 3

To the cooking pot, add potatoes, sauteed onions, chicken soup base, turmeric, black pepper, white pepper, cayenne pepper, curry powder, and soy sauce, and cook until potatoes are tender.

- Step 4

Add whole milk and a half and half cream and bring back to boil. Add instant potato flakes, stirring until well blended. Adjust seasonings to taste. Garnish with chopped chives or green onions.

Nutrition Facts

---

198 calories; protein 6.7g; carbohydrates 25.9g; fat 8.1g; cholesterol 8.5mg; sodium 1167mg

---

Harvey's Moroccan Roast Chicken

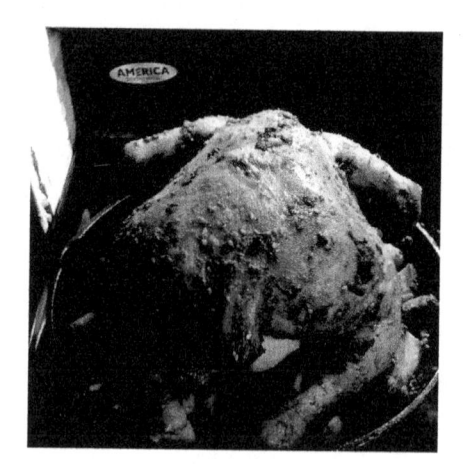

Paprika, fresh mint, and lemon make the best rub for this roast chicken. It roasts slowly under the foil and turns out so juicy and flavorful.

Prep time: 20 mins

Servings: 4 servings

Ingredients

Dry Spice Mix:

- ⅛ teaspoon ground cloves
- ¼ teaspoon ground black pepper
- ⅜ teaspoon fennel seed, ground
- ¾ teaspoon sesame seeds, ground
- ⅛ teaspoon ground coriander
- ⅛ teaspoon ground cumin
- ⅛ teaspoon ground allspice
- ¼ teaspoon ground nutmeg
- ¾ teaspoon ground ginger
- ⅛ teaspoon ground cardamom

Spice Paste:

- 2 tablespoons Hungarian paprika
- ¼ cup fresh lemon juice
- 1 tablespoon salt
- 3 tablespoons chopped fresh mint
- 1 teaspoon ground black pepper
- 2 cloves garlic, peeled and crushed
- 3 tablespoons olive oil
- 1 pound small red potatoes, quartered
- 2 cups baby carrots

- 2 small lemons
- 1 (4 pounds) of roasted chicken, rinsed and patted dry

Directions

- **Step 1**

Preheat oven to 350 degrees F (175 degrees C).

- **Step 2**

For the spice mix: Mix together in a bowl the cloves, pepper, fennel, sesame seeds, coriander, cumin, allspice, nutmeg, ginger, and cardamom. Set aside.

- **Step 3**

For the spice paste: Place the paprika, lemon juice, the spice mix (from Step 2), salt, chopped mint, black pepper, and garlic cloves in a blender. Add 2 tablespoons of olive oil and blend until ingredients are mixed about 6 or 8 pulses. Slowly add the additional olive oil if the mixture seems too thick to spread. Blend just until the mixture is a smooth paste.

- **Step 4**

Spread potatoes and carrots in a roasting pan. Rub about 1/4 of the spice paste inside the cavity of the chicken. Rub the remainder of the paste on the outside of the chicken, including the underside. Place the chicken directly on the carrots and potatoes. Pierce the 2 lemons all over with a fork and place them into the chicken cavity.

- **Step 5**

Tent the chicken with aluminum foil. Roast approximately 2 hours until the thickest part of the thigh reaches 180 degrees F (80 degrees C) and the juices run clear. Remove from the oven and let rest for about 10 minutes before serving.

Nutrition Facts

789 calories; protein 64.9g; carbohydrates 32.7g; fat 45.2g; cholesterol 194.1mg; sodium 1993mg

Israeli Moroccan Couscous

The vegetables can be cubed but will take longer to cook.

Prep time: 20 mins
Servings: 8 servings

Ingredients

- 1 tablespoon olive oil
- 1 onion, diced
- 3 cups vegetable broth
- 2 carrots, peeled and julienned
- 2 turnips, peeled and julienned
- 1 sweet potato, julienned
- 1 zucchini, julienned
- 1 red bell pepper, julienned
- 1 (15 ounces) of can garbanzo beans, drained
- 1 (15 ounces) of can tomato sauce
- ¼ teaspoon ground cinnamon
- ½ teaspoon ground turmeric
- 1 pinch saffron
- 1 pinch curry powder
- 2 cups uncooked couscous

Directions

- Step 1

Heat oil in a large pot over medium-high heat; saute onion until golden. Pour in vegetable broth and bring to a boil. Stir in carrots, turnips, and sweet potato. Reduce heat to medium and simmer 15 minutes.

- Step 2

Reduce heat to low and add zucchini and red bell pepper. Simmer for 20 minutes.

- Step 3

Stir in garbanzo beans, tomato sauce, cinnamon, turmeric, saffron, and curry powder. Simmer until heated through.

- Step 4

Meanwhile, bring 2 1/2 cups of water to a boil. Stir in couscous, cover, and remove from heat. Let stand 5 to 7 minutes. Fluff with a fork and serve with vegetables on top.

Nutrition Facts

282 calories; protein 9.4g; carbohydrates 55.2g; fat 2.8g; sodium 634.3mg

Vegetarian Moroccan Harira

Harira is a famous Moroccan soup, and here's a hearty

ABDUL AZIZ

vegetarian (and vegan!) version - packed with tomatoes and chickpeas and flavored with paprika, turmeric, saffron, ginger, and harissa. The amount of water can be adjusted depending on the thickness you want.

Prep time: 20 mins
Servings: 5 servings

Ingredients

- 2 tablespoons vegetable oil
- 1 large onion, chopped
- 2 pounds tomatoes, diced
- 1 (15 ounce) can chickpeas, drained
- 1 bunch fresh cilantro, chopped
- 1 bunch fresh parsley, chopped
- 20 fresh mint leaves, chopped
- 1 teaspoon ground paprika
- 1 teaspoon ground turmeric
- 1 teaspoon ground ginger
- ½ teaspoon harissa
- 1 pinch saffron threads
- 4 cups water, or more to taste
- 1 tablespoon all-purpose flour
- 1 teaspoon cornstarch
- ½ cup cherry tomatoes halved
- salt and ground black pepper to taste

Directions

- **Step 1**

Heat oil in a large pot over medium heat and cook onion until soft and translucent, about 5 minutes. Add tomatoes, chickpeas, cilantro, parsley, mint, paprika, turmeric, ginger, harissa, and saffron. Add water and cook over medium heat until flavors have combined for about 30 minutes.

- **Step 2**

Mix a few tablespoons of soup liquid with flour and cornstarch in a small bowl and return to the soup, stirring in well. Add cherry tomatoes. Bring to a boil, reduce heat, and simmer over low heat until soup thickens about 10 minutes. Season with salt and pepper.

Note

If you have time, peel your tomatoes. To do this, cut an X on the bottom of each, submerge in boiling water for 25 seconds, transfer to an ice water bath, then peel gently and dice.

Nutrition Facts

182 calories; protein 5.7g; carbohydrates 27.1g; fat 6.9g; sodium 231.1mg

Moroccan Mashed Potatoes

These creamy Middle Eastern-style potatoes are flavored with turmeric and use olive oil rather than butter. They are great alone and for fillings in puff pastries. Amounts of salt, pepper, and other spices may be adjusted to taste.

Prep time: 20 mins
Servings: 32 servings

Ingredients

- 10 large baking potatoes, peeled and cubed
- 3 tablespoons olive oil, or as needed
- 1 onion, diced
- 1 tablespoon ground turmeric
- 1 tablespoon salt, or to taste
- 2 teaspoons ground black pepper
- ½ teaspoon ground cumin

Directions

- **Step 1**

Place the potatoes into a large pot, and fill with enough water to cover. Bring to a boil over medium-high heat, cook until tender, and be pierced with a fork, about 20 minutes.

- **Step 2**

Meanwhile, place 1 tablespoon olive oil in a skillet and heat over medium-high heat. Stir in the onion and cook until translucent and lightly browned, about 6 minutes.

- **Step 3**

Drain water from the potatoes and mash. Stir in the onion, and continue mashing. Mix in the turmeric, salt, pepper, and cumin. Add the remaining 2 tablespoons olive oil, or amount desired to make the potatoes more or less creamy.

Nutrition Facts

---

103 calories; protein 1.8g; carbohydrates 21.3g; fat 1.4g; sodium 223.6mg

---

Tempeh Kabobs with Moroccan Couscous

Soaked in a delicious honey-soy marinade and paired with grilled vegetables, these kabobs will please both meat-eaters and vegetarians.

Prep time: 30 mins
Servings: 4 servings

Ingredients

- 1 (8 ounces) of package tempeh, cut into 1/2 inch squares
- 16 fresh white mushrooms
- 1 medium eggplant, cut into 1-inch cubes
- 1 large red bell pepper, cut into 1-inch pieces
- 16 cherry tomatoes
- 8 tablespoons olive oil
- 4 tablespoons soy sauce
- 4 tablespoons teriyaki sauce
- 3 tablespoons honey
- 1 tablespoon grated fresh ginger root
- 1 tablespoon chopped fresh garlic
- salt and pepper to taste
- 2 cups vegetable broth
- 1 tablespoon grated fresh ginger root
- 1 teaspoon ground cumin
- salt to taste
- 1 cup dry couscous
- ¾ cup raisins
- ¾ cup drained canned chickpeas (garbanzo beans)
- 1 lemon

Directions

- **Step 1**

Place tempeh, mushrooms, eggplant, red bell pepper, and cherry tomatoes in a large resealable plastic bag. In a mixing bowl, whisk together olive oil, soy sauce, teriyaki sauce, and honey; season with 1 tablespoon ginger, 1 tablespoon garlic, and salt and pepper to taste. Pour mixture over tempeh and veggies, seal, and shake to coat. Refrigerate for 2 hours.

- Step 2

Preheat grill for medium-high heat. Thread tempeh and veggies on skewers. Reserve remaining marinade.

- Step 3

Grill skewers, often turning to make sure everything is cooked evenly. These can also be done in the broiler.

- Step 4

While grilling kabobs, combine vegetable stock, 1 tablespoon grated ginger, cumin, and salt. Bring to a light boil. Stir in couscous, raisins, and garbanzo beans; cover and remove from heat. Let sit for five minutes, or until fluffy. Just before serving, squeeze lemon over couscous and stir. Serve kabobs with reserved marinade.

Nutrition Facts

820 calories; protein 26.8g; carbohydrates 110.1g; fat 35.3g; sodium 2131.8mg

Moroccan Shabbat Fish

Prep time: 20 mins
Servings: 6 servings

Ingredients

- 1 red bell pepper, cut into thin strips
- 3 tomatoes, sliced
- 6 (6 ounces) of tilapia fillets
- 2 tablespoons paprika
- 1 tablespoon chicken bouillon granules
- 1 teaspoon cayenne pepper
- salt and pepper to taste
- ¼ cup olive oil
- 1 cup water
- ¼ cup chopped fresh parsley

Directions

- **Step 1**

Preheat an oven to 200 degrees F (95 degrees C).

- **Step 2**

Layer the sliced red peppers and sliced tomatoes in the bottom of a baking dish. Arrange the tilapia fillets on top of the vegetables.

- **Step 3**

Combine the paprika, chicken bouillon, cayenne, salt, pepper, olive oil, and water and mix well. Pour the seasoning mixture over the fish. Sprinkle with parsley.

- **Step 4**

Cover the baking dish with aluminum foil and bake in the preheated oven until the fish flakes easily with a fork and the vegetables are tender for about 1 hour.

Nutrition Facts

278 calories; protein 35.9g; carbohydrates 5.9g; fat 12g; cholesterol 62.3mg; sodium 303.1mg

Moroccan Meat Cigars

This goes great with hummus on the side!

Prep time: 20 mins
  Servings: 4 servings

∽

Ingredients

- 1 teaspoon olive oil
- ½ pound lean ground beef
- ½ cup canned crushed tomatoes, drained
- ¼ teaspoon ground cinnamon
- ¼ teaspoon ground cumin
- ⅛ teaspoon paprika
- ⅛ teaspoon ground allspice
- 1 (16 ounces) of package phyllo dough

- cooking oil spray

Directions

- **Step 1**

Preheat oven to 350 degrees F (175 degrees C). Lightly grease a baking sheet.

- **Step 2**

Heat olive oil in a skillet over medium-high heat. Cook ground beef until it loses its pink color and begins to brown. Drain fat from skillet. Add tomatoes, cinnamon, cumin, paprika, and allspice. Reduce heat to medium and simmer until mixture reduces slightly about 10 minutes.

- **Step 3**

Remove one phyllo sheet from the package and keep the rest covered with a clean cloth until ready to use. On a flat work surface, cut the phyllo sheet into 2 14x9-inch rectangles. Spray the first half-sheet with cooking spray, place the 2nd half on top of it and spray again with oil. Place a generous teaspoon of the meat mixture near the narrow end of the dough. Fold dough over the top of the meat, fold in the sides of the dough, and roll into a narrow tube (cigar) shape. Repeat until all the meat has been rolled up. Arrange cigars on a prepared baking sheet.

- **Step 4**

Bake in preheated oven until lightly browned, about 25 minutes.

Nutrition Facts

460 calories; protein 19g; carbohydrates 60.4g; fat 14.9g; cholesterol 37mg; sodium 620mg

Vegetarian Moroccan Stew

A great vegetarian meal that's really easy to make. Serve over steamed couscous.

Prep time: 15 mins
Servings: 6 servings

Ingredients

- 1 tablespoon olive oil
- 1 yellow onion, diced
- 4 cloves garlic, minced
- 2 teaspoons ground cumin
- 1 (4 inches) of cinnamon stick
- salt and pepper to taste
- 1 pound butternut squash - peeled, seeded, and cut into 2-inch cubes
- 4 large red potatoes, cut into 2-inch cubes
- 2 cups vegetable broth
- 1 (15 ounces) of can garbanzo beans, drained
- 1 (14.5 ounces) of can canned diced tomatoes with their juice
- 1 cup pitted, brine-cured green olives
- ½ teaspoon lemon zest
- 1 ¾ cups water
- 1 (10 ounces) box of uncooked couscous
- 6 tablespoons plain yogurt
- 6 tablespoons chopped fresh cilantro

Directions

- Step 1

Heat olive oil in a large covered saucepan or Dutch oven over medium heat until oil is hot but not smoking. Drop in the onion, garlic, cumin, cinnamon stick, and salt and pepper. Cook and stir for 5 minutes until onion is tender and translucent.

- Step 2

Stir in the butternut squash and potato cubes, broth, garbanzo beans, and tomatoes, bringing the mixture to a boil. Reduce heat, cover the pot, and simmer about 20 minutes, occasionally stirring, until the squash and potatoes are tender. Remove the stew from heat, and stir in the olives and lemon zest.

- Step 3

In a large saucepan, bring 1 3/4 cup water to a boil. Stir in couscous. Cover and remove from the heat; let stand for 5 minutes. Fluff with a fork; cool. Serve stew over cooked couscous. Garnish each serving with a dollop of yogurt and a sprinkle of cilantro leaves.

Nutrition Facts

494 calories; protein 14.8g; carbohydrates 97g; fat 7.1g; cholesterol 0.9mg; sodium 990.1mg.

Moroccan Black-Eyed Peas (Cowpeas)

This delicious Moroccan-style recipe smells so good while cooking and tastes so yummy.

Prep time: 10 mins

Servings: 8 servings

∼

Ingredients

- 1 ½ cups dried black-eyed peas (cowpeas)
- 1 onion, chopped
- 1 (8 ounces) of can tomato sauce
- ½ cup olive oil
- ¼ cup chopped fresh cilantro
- 3 cloves garlic, finely chopped
- 1 ½ teaspoons salt
- 1 ½ teaspoon of ground cumin
- 1 ½ teaspoon of sweet paprika
- 1 teaspoon ground ginger
- ¼ teaspoon cayenne pepper
- 3 ½ cups water, or more if needed

Directions

- **Step 1**

Place black-eyed peas into a large container and cover with several inches of cool water; let stand for 8 hours to overnight. Drain and rinse peas.

- **Step 2**

Combine peas, onion, tomato sauce, olive oil, cilantro, garlic, salt, cumin, paprika, ginger, and cayenne pepper in a stockpot; pour 3 1/2 cups water over pea mixture. Bring water to a boil, decrease the heat to low, cover pot, and simmer, stirring occasionally and adding more water if the sauce gets too thick until peas are tender about 1 1/2 hours.

Note

If using fresh-picked peas, omit the soaking process and reduce the cooking time by half.

Fresh parsley can be substituted for fresh cilantro. Hungarian paprika can be substituted for sweet paprika.

Quick-soak method for peas: add washed peas to the pot of boiling water; immediately remove from heat and soak for 1 to 1 1/2 hours.

Nutrition Facts

242 calories; protein 8.1g; carbohydrates 22.6g; fat 14.1g; sodium 593.4mg.

Moroccan Sweet Potato Stew

A perfect blend of rich sweet potato stew with a kick of curry powder and ginger plus the crunch of peanuts.

Prep time: 25 mins
Servings: 6 servings

∼

Ingredients

- 3 cups peeled and cubed sweet potatoes
- 3 cups vegetable broth, divided
- 2 teaspoons olive oil
- 1 cup chopped onion
- 1 stalk celery, chopped
- ½ cup chopped red bell pepper
- 1 clove garlic, minced, or more to taste
- 1 (15 ounces) of can chickpeas, drained and rinsed
- 1 (14.5 ounces) of can diced tomatoes, drained
- 1 tablespoon lemon juice

- 2 teaspoons fresh grated ginger
- 1 teaspoon ground cumin
- 1 teaspoon curry powder
- 1 teaspoon ground coriander
- 1 teaspoon chili powder
- ½ teaspoon salt
- ¼ teaspoon pepper
- ½ cup raisins
- 2 tablespoons peanut butter

Directions

- **Step 1**

Place sweet potatoes in a microwave-safe bowl and add a splash of the broth. Cook in the microwave until slightly softened, 3 to 5 minutes.

- **Step 2**

Heat olive oil in a soup pot over medium heat. Add onion, celery, bell pepper, and garlic. Cook and stir for 3 to 5 minutes. Add softened sweet potatoes, remaining broth, chickpeas, tomatoes, lemon juice, ginger, cumin, curry powder, coriander, chili powder, salt, and pepper. Bring to a boil, reduce heat, and cover the pot. Simmer soup until vegetables are tender, about 20 minutes.

- **Step 3**

Stir raisins and peanut butter into the soup and simmer 5 minutes more. Adjust spices if necessary.

Nutrition Facts

252 calories; protein 6.9g; carbohydrates 45.4g; fat 5.5g; sodium 745mg.

Moroccan Shepherd's Pie

This is a Moroccan take on shepherd's pie. Delicious combinations of savory and sweet, with lamb and turmeric simmered with cinnamon, raisins, and sweet potato. This dish also looks pleasant, and each happy eater gets their own ramekin!

Prep time: 20 mins
Servings: 4 servings

∼

Ingredients

- cooking spray

- 1 tablespoon olive oil
- 1 pound cubed lamb stew meat
- 1 teaspoon ground cumin, divided
- ½ teaspoon salt, divided
- 1 ½ cups chopped onion
- 4 garlic cloves, minced
- 1 tablespoon tomato paste
- 1 ½ (10.5 ounces) of cans low-sodium chicken broth
- ½ cup water
- 2 tablespoons olives, or to taste
- ⅓ cup raisins
- 2 tablespoons honey
- ½ teaspoon cayenne pepper
- ¼ teaspoon ground turmeric
- ½ teaspoon ground cinnamon, divided
- 1 cup frozen green peas
- 4 cups peeled and chopped sweet potatoes
- 1 large egg, lightly beaten

Directions

- **Step 1**

Preheat oven to 350 degrees F (175 degrees C). Spray four 10-ounce ramekins with cooking spray.

- **Step 2**

Heat a large skillet over medium-high heat. Add oil to pan; swirl to coat.

- **Step 3**

Sprinkle lamb evenly with 1/2 teaspoon cumin and 1/4 teaspoon salt. Cook and stir lamb in the hot oil until browned on all sides, about 4 minutes. Transfer lamb to a bowl. Cook and stir onion in the same skillet until slightly softened about 3 minutes; add garlic and cook until fragrant, about 30 seconds.

- Step 4

Stir tomato paste into onion mixture until evenly coated, about 30 seconds. Pour broth and water into onion mixture; bring to a boil, scraping skillet with a wooden spoon to loosen browned bits of food. Return lamb to skillet.

- Step 5

Stir remaining 1/2 teaspoon cumin, olives, raisins, honey, cayenne pepper, turmeric, and 1/8 teaspoon cinnamon into lamb mixture. Reduce heat and simmer, occasionally stirring, until lamb is fully cooked and flavors have blended for about 30 minutes. Remove from heat and stir in peas.

- Step 6

Place sweet potatoes into a large pot and cover with salted water; bring to a boil. Reduce heat to medium-low and simmer until tender, about 10 minutes. Drain and cool for 5 minutes. Transfer sweet potatoes to a bowl and sprinkle with 1/4 teaspoon salt and 3/8 teaspoon cinnamon. Beat potato mixture with a hand mixer at high speed until smooth. Add egg; beat until incorporated.

- Step 7

Spoon lamb mixture into each ramekin; spread sweet potato mixture over lamb mixture. Place ramekins on a baking sheet.

- **Step 8**

Bake in the preheated oven until bubbling, about 25 minutes.

Nutrition Facts

---

425 calories; protein 25.5g; carbohydrates 60.3g; fat 10.2g; cholesterol 101.8mg; sodium 586.3mg

---

Moroccan Chicken Sann

The marinade is incredible, and the pieces of prune and apricot create a nice sweet balance. Serve with Basmati rice.

Prep time: 15 mins

ABDUL AZIZ

Servings: 6 servings

Ingredients

- ½ cup soy sauce
- ½ cup fresh lemon juice
- ½ cup sherry
- ½ cup honey
- ½ teaspoon ground thyme
- 2 teaspoons curry powder
- ½ teaspoon dried oregano
- ½ teaspoon ground ginger
- ½ teaspoon ground black pepper
- 1 clove garlic, pressed
- 3 pounds cut up chicken pieces
- 1 ½ cups uncooked brown rice
- 3 cups water
- 2 tablespoons olive oil
- 8 pitted prunes
- 8 dried apricot halves

Directions

- Step 1

Whisk together the soy sauce, lemon juice, sherry, honey, thyme, curry powder, dried oregano, ground ginger, ground black pepper, and garlic. Place the marinade with the chicken into a resealable bag, and marinate for at least 30 minutes or up to 24 hours.

- **Step 2**

Bring the brown rice and water to a boil in a saucepan over high heat. Reduce the heat to medium-low, cover, and simmer until the rice is tender and the liquid has been absorbed for about 45 to 50 minutes.

- **Step 3**

Heat the olive oil in a large skillet over medium-high heat, and cook the chicken pieces until browned on all sides. Sprinkle the chicken with prunes and apricots; pour the marinade into the skillet. Bring to a simmer, cover, and cook for 30 minutes. Uncover and simmer until the sauce is slightly thickened, the chicken is no longer pink at the bone, and the juices run clear for about 15 minutes. An instant-read thermometer inserted near the bone should read 165 degrees F (74 degrees C). Serve over the brown rice.

Nutrition Facts

681 calories; protein 36.6g; carbohydrates 82.2g; fat 23.1g; cholesterol 97mg; sodium 1424.7mg

Moroccan Eggplant Dip

Serve this to folks who never eat eggplant. They will be amazed. Serve at room temperature with wheat crackers.

Prep time: 20 mins
Servings: 12 servings

Ingredients

- 1 (8 ounces) of can tomato sauce
- ¼ cup red wine vinegar
- 1 tablespoon ground cumin
- 1 teaspoon salt
- 1 teaspoon white sugar
- ¼ teaspoon ground cayenne
- 2 tablespoons olive oil
- 2 cloves garlic, minced
- 1 ½ pounds eggplant, unpeeled, cut into chunks

- 1 red bell pepper, seeded, and cut into chunks
- ½ cup chopped fresh cilantro

Directions

- **Step 1**

Mix tomato sauce, red wine vinegar, cumin, salt, sugar, and cayenne together in a small bowl.

- **Step 2**

Heat olive oil in a large skillet over medium-low heat. Add garlic; cook and stir until golden, about 2 minutes. Add eggplant and red bell pepper; pour in tomato sauce mixture. Simmer, covered, until eggplant and red bell pepper soften, about 20 minutes. Remove from heat and let cool, about 10 minutes.

- **Step 3**

Transfer eggplant mixture to a food processor; pulse until it reaches the desired consistency. Sprinkle cilantro over dip.

Nutrition Facts

47 calories; protein 1.1g; carbohydrates 6g; fat 2.6g; sodium 295mg.

Cold Roasted Moroccan Spiced Salmon

This easy dry rub blasts the fish with a unique Middle Eastern flair and is perfectly paired with other cold sides and salads. Roast it in the morning to enjoy cold with your guests that evening. Any variety of salmon, or even trout, works; cooking time remains the same as long as the cut is about one inch thick. It may seem like a lot of seasonings to use on one cut of meat, but cold meat can lose flavor, so the idea is to blast it with flavors from the beginning. If cold fish isn't your thing, refrigerate it and bring it to room temperature to serve.

Prep time: 15 mins
Servings: 6 servings

∼

Ingredients

- ¾ teaspoon ground cinnamon
- ¾ teaspoon ground cumin
- ½ teaspoon salt
- ½ teaspoon ground ginger
- ¼ teaspoon mustard powder
- ¼ teaspoon ground nutmeg
- ⅛ teaspoon cayenne pepper
- ⅛ teaspoon ground allspice
- 2 teaspoons white sugar
- 2 pounds (1-inch thick) boneless, skin-on center-cut salmon fillets
- 1 tablespoon fresh lime juice

Directions

- Step 1

In a small bowl, combine the cinnamon, cumin, salt, ginger, mustard, nutmeg, cayenne, allspice, and sugar; set aside.

- Step 2

Line a baking sheet with foil, then spray with nonstick cooking spray. Rinse the salmon with cold water and pat dry. Lightly sprinkle the skin with the spice mix, then place the salmon skin-side down on the prepared baking sheet. Sprinkle the remaining spice mix evenly over the salmon. Allow the salmon to come to room temperature, 30 to 40 minutes.

- Step 3

Preheat oven to 425 degrees F (220 degrees C).

- Step 4

Sprinkle the salmon with lime juice and roast in the oven for 12 minutes. Remove from oven and allow to stand at room temperature for 15 minutes. The salmon will still be rare when removed from the oven but will continue to cook as it rests. After 15 minutes, wrap the fish tightly with foil and refrigerate for at least 2 hours before serving.

Nutrition Facts

---

225 calories; protein 30.2g; carbohydrates 2.2g; fat 9.8g; cholesterol 83.9mg; sodium 260.6mg

---

Moroccan Chicken and Whole Grain Couscous

A flavorful chicken stew that uses exotic spices and nice vegetables served over whole-grain couscous. This recipe was actually a real chicken contest winner! Vegetables and even meat

can vary according to taste, but I find squash, carrots, bell peppers, and lamb work well in this recipe. Even though the spices seem strange, the flavors are subtle but fragrant! A real favorite at home.

Prep time: 15 mins
Servings: 6 servings

∼

Ingredients

- 1 cup whole wheat couscous
- 1 tablespoon vegetable oil
- 1 medium onion, chopped
- 2 bay leaves
- 5 whole cloves, crushed
- ½ teaspoon cinnamon
- 1 teaspoon ground dried turmeric
- ¼ teaspoon ground cayenne pepper
- 6 skinless, boneless chicken breast halves - chopped
- 1 (16 ounces) of can garbanzo beans
- 1 (16 ounces) of can crushed tomatoes
- 1 (48 fluid ounce) of can chicken broth
- 2 carrots, cut into 1/2 inch pieces
- 1 zucchini, cut into 1/2-inch pieces
- salt to taste

Directions

- **Step 1**

Prepare the couscous according to package directions.

- **Step 2**

Heat the oil in a large pot over medium heat, and cook onion until tender. Mix in bay leaves, cloves, cinnamon, turmeric, and cayenne pepper. Place chicken in the pot, and cook until well browned. Pour garbanzo beans, tomatoes, and broth into the pot, and bring to a boil. Reduce heat to low, and simmer 25 minutes.

- **Step 3**

Mix carrots and zucchini into the pot. Season with salt. Continue cooking for 10 minutes or until vegetables are tender. Serve stew over cooked couscous.

Nutrition Facts

---

399 calories; protein 33.4g; carbohydrates 50.7g; fat 6.7g; cholesterol 66.8mg; sodium 1539mg

---

Moroccan-Style Chicken with Butternut Squash Noodles

Delicious Moroccan-inspired chicken dish served with butternut squash noodles.

Prep time: 25 mins
Servings: 6 servings

~

Ingredients

- 2 cups spiralized butternut squash
- 3 tablespoons olive oil, divided
- salt and ground black pepper to taste
- 2 tablespoons butter
- 1 ½ pound of skinless, boneless chicken breasts, thinly sliced

- 1 teaspoon Moroccan spice mix (such as McCormick®), or to taste
- ½ cup orange juice
- ¼ cup chopped dried apricots
- ¼ cup dried cranberries
- ¼ cup chopped dates
- ¼ cup almond slivers
- 2 cups cooked rice

Direction

- Step 1

Preheat the oven to 400 degrees F (200 degrees C).

- Step 2

Place spiralized butternut squash in a bowl; add 1 tablespoon oil, salt, and pepper. Toss to coat and transfer to a baking sheet.

- Step 3

Bake in the preheated oven until just tender, 7 to 10 minutes.

- Step 4

Heat butter and the remaining 2 tablespoons oil in a large saute pan over medium-high heat. Add chicken and sprinkle both sides with Moroccan spice, salt, and pepper to taste. Cover pan and cook, occasionally turning, until chicken is no longer pink in the center and the juices run clear, 5 to 7 minutes. Remove chicken and set aside.

- **Step 5**

Add orange juice, apricots, cranberries, and dates to the same saute pan over medium heat. Cook and stir until orange juice thickens, 3 to 4 minutes. Add almonds and toss to coat. Remove topping from heat.

- **Step 6**

Plate each portion with butternut squash, cooked rice, chicken, and topping.

Note

If you don't have a spiralizer, you can roast the squash and cut it into cubes instead.

Nutrition Facts

402 calories; protein 27.2g; carbohydrates 36.8g; fat 16.5g; cholesterol 74.6mg; sodium 113.4mg

Moroccan Salmon Cakes with Garlic Mayonnaise

This is a great alternative to the standard salmon patty recipe using couscous, spinach, and cumin for an exotic flavor.

Prep time: 20 mins
Servings: 4 to 5 servings

Ingredients

Garlic mayonnaise:

- ½ cup mayonnaise
- 1 clove garlic, crushed
- ⅛ teaspoon paprika

Salmon cakes:

- ½ cup couscous
- ⅔ cup orange juice
- 1 (14.75 ounces) of can red salmon, drained
- 1 (10 ounces) of package frozen chopped spinach - thawed, drained, and squeezed dry
- 2 egg yolks, beaten

- 2 cloves garlic, crushed
- 1 teaspoon ground cumin
- ½ teaspoon ground black pepper
- ½ teaspoon salt
- 3 tablespoons olive oil

Directions

- **Step 1**

In a small stainless steel or glass bowl, stir together mayonnaise, garlic, and paprika. Set aside.

- **Step 2**

Prepare couscous according to package directions using the 2/3 cup of orange juice in place of water.

- **Step 3**

In a mixing bowl, combine the cooked couscous, red salmon, drained spinach, egg yolks, garlic, cumin, black pepper, and salt. Form into patties.

- **Step 4**

In a large skillet over medium heat, heat the olive oil and fry patties until golden brown, turning once, about 8 to 10 minutes. Serve with garlic mayonnaise.

Nutrition Fact

620 calories; protein 28.8g; carbohydrates 26.4g; fat 46.4g; cholesterol 178.4mg; sodium 950.1mg

Moroccan Potato Casserole

This is a very colorful dish and a very tasty one. A dressing made from fresh herbs and spices gives this vegetable dish a Moroccan flavor. It is a great vegan recipe!

Prep time: 40 mins
Servings: 6 servings

Ingredients

- 6 cloves garlic
- salt to taste
- 2 teaspoons paprika
- ½ teaspoon ground cumin
- ¼ teaspoon ground cayenne pepper
- ¾ cup chopped fresh cilantro
- ¾ cup chopped parsley
- 1 lemon, juiced
- 3 tablespoons red wine vinegar
- 3 tablespoons olive oil
- 1 ½ pound of red potatoes, sliced 1/2 inch thick
- 1 large red bell pepper, cut into 1-inch pieces
- 1 yellow bell pepper, cut into 1 1/2 inch squares
- 1 large green bell pepper, cut into 1 1/2 inch pieces
- 4 stalks celery, cut into 2-inch pieces
- 1 pound tomatoes, each cut into 8 wedges
- 2 tablespoons olive oil

Directions

- **Step 1**

Preheat oven to 350 degrees F (175 degrees C).

- **Step 2**

Combine garlic, 1/2 teaspoon salt, paprika, cumin, and cayenne in a food processor bowl. Process until mixture forms a paste. Add herbs, and pulse a few times to blend. Add lemon juice, vinegar, and 2 to 3 tablespoons olive oil; blend. Season to taste with salt.

- **Step 3**

In a large bowl, combine potatoes, peppers, and celery. Season with salt, and toss with herb sauce. Transfer to a large shallow baking dish. Scatter tomatoes among the potato mixture. Drizzle 1 to 2 tablespoons oil over the top, and cover with foil.

- **Step 4**

Bake for 35 minutes. Remove foil. Continue baking until vegetables are tender, 20 to 30 minutes. Serve warm.

Nutrition Facts

237 calories; protein 4.7g; carbohydrates 30.9g; fat 12.1g; sodium 44.5mg.

Moroccan Chicken Thigh Sheet Pan Dinner

This Moroccan-inspired sheet pan dinner is packed with bold sweet and savory flavors and palate-pleasing textures. This is perfect for quick weeknight dinners or laid-back dinner parties. Ras el hanout is a North African seasoning available in specialty grocery stores, or if you'd like to make your own, there are many recipes available online.

Prep time: 30 mins
Servings: 4 servings

Ingredients

- 1 lemon, zested and juiced
- 2 tablespoons olive oil
- 1 ½ teaspoon of ras el hanout
- ½ teaspoon salt
- 4 (6 ounces) of bone-in chicken thighs with skin
- 1 medium sweet potato, peeled and cut into 1-inch chunks
- 1 medium zucchini, cut into 1-inch chunks
- 1 (15 ounces) of can chickpeas, drained and rinsed
- 1 (14 ounces) of can quartered artichoke hearts, drained
- 1 teaspoon ras el hanout
- ½ teaspoon salt
- 2 tablespoons olive oil
- ¼ cup pomegranate seeds
- ¼ cup chopped fresh parsley
- 2 tablespoons shelled pistachios, coarsely chopped

Directions

- **Step 1**

Combine lemon juice, lemon zest, 2 tablespoons olive oil, 1 1/2 teaspoons ras el hanout, and 1/2 teaspoon salt in a resealable plastic bag. Place chicken thighs into the bag, making sure marinade gets under the skin. Seal and refrigerate for at least 30 minutes. Remove chicken from refrigerator 20 minutes before baking and let it come to room temperature.

- **Step 2**

Preheat the oven to 400 degrees F (200 degrees C).

- **Step 3**

Combine sweet potato, zucchini, chickpeas, and artichoke hearts in a bowl. Sprinkle with 1 teaspoon ras el hanout and 1/2 teaspoon salt. Drizzle with 2 tablespoons olive oil and stir to combine evenly.

- **Step 4**

Remove chicken from marinade and place on a 13x18-inch rimmed sheet pan. Place vegetable mixture around chicken.

- **Step 5**

Bake in the preheated oven, flipping vegetables halfway through, or until chicken has reached an internal temperature of 165 degrees F (74 degrees C), about 30 minutes.

- **Step 6**

Remove from oven and garnish with pomegranate seeds, parsley, and pistachios before serving.

Notes

To make cleanup easier, line the sheet pan with aluminum foil.

Place pistachios into a small resealable storage bag and crush with a rolling pin or meat tenderizer.

The sweet potato used for this recipe weighed about 14 ounces.

Nutrition Facts

648 calories; protein 33.2g; carbohydrates 52.6g; fat 35.4g; cholesterol 105.8mg; sodium 1539.9mg.

Lamb Chops with Preserved Lemon (Moroccan Style)

The preserved lemon in this extremely tasty dish brings out the full flavor of the lamb! These lamb chops can be served on a bed of couscous, with tabbouleh as a side dish. Enjoy with a wine of your choice, keeping in mind that this dish is quite spicy and has the tang of the preserved lemon. A medium white such as chardonnay or even a Mosel is preferred. A mild to sweet red wine would also be great.

Prep time: 35 mins
Servings: 4 servings

Ingredients

- ¼ cup chopped fresh cilantro
- ¼ cup chopped fresh parsley

- ¼ cup chopped fresh mint
- 4 cloves garlic, minced
- ¼ cup chopped Moroccan preserved lemon
- 1 tablespoon olive oil
- ground black pepper to taste
- 1 (7 bone) rack of lamb, trimmed and frenched
- ¼ cup slivered kalamata olives
- 1 red bell pepper, thinly sliced

Directions

- **Step 1**

Stir cilantro, parsley, and mint together in a small saucepan. Remove half of the herb mixture, and set aside. Stir the garlic, lemon, olives, olive oil, and black pepper into the remaining herbs. Spread 2 tablespoons of this mixture onto the lamb rack. Wrap the exposed bones with aluminum foil to keep them from burning. Stir the olives and bell pepper into the reserved mixture and keep warm over low heat.

- **Step 2**

Preheat an outdoor grill for medium heat.

- **Step 3**

Cook the lamb rack on the preheated grill until cooked to the desired degree of doneness, about 4 minutes per side for medium-rare. Baste occasionally with the warmed relish. Once cooked, remove from grill, and allow it to rest for 5 minutes before slicing into individual chops.

- **Step 4**

To serve, arrange lamb chops on a platter, spoon some of the warmed relishes over them, and sprinkle with the reserved chopped herbs.

Nutrition Facts

425 calories; protein 21.6g; carbohydrates 5.1g; fat 35g; cholesterol 95.1mg; sodium 1026.5mg.

Slow Cooker Root Vegetable Tagine

This is a subtly spiced, super easy slow cooker meal. A good introduction to Moroccan food. Serve with couscous.

Prep time: 50 mins
Servings: 8 servings

Ingredients

- 1 pound parsnips, peeled and diced
- 1 pound turnips, peeled and diced
- 2 medium onions, chopped
- 1 pound carrots, peeled and diced
- 6 dried apricots, chopped
- 4 pitted prunes, chopped
- 1 teaspoon ground turmeric
- 1 teaspoon ground cumin
- ½ teaspoon ground ginger
- ½ teaspoon ground cinnamon
- ¼ teaspoon ground cayenne pepper
- 1 tablespoon dried parsley
- 1 tablespoon dried cilantro
- 1 (14 ounces) of can vegetable broth

Directions

- Step 1

In a slow cooker, toss together the parsnips, turnips, onions, carrots, apricots, and prunes. Season with turmeric, cumin, ginger, cinnamon, cayenne pepper, parsley, and cilantro. Pour in the vegetable broth.

- Step 2

Cover and cook 9 hours on low.

Nutrition Fact

---

131 calories; protein 2.8g; carbohydrates 31g; fat 0.7g; sodium 187.4mg.

Moroccan-Spiced Roasted Carrots

Roasted carrots with the Moroccan spice blend. Fast and easy, and pairs well with any meat!

Prep time: 10 mins
Servings: 6 servings

∽

Ingredients

- 2 pounds carrots, cut into thick slices

- ¼ cup olive oil
- 2 tablespoons lemon juice
- 2 teaspoons white sugar
- 1 teaspoon ground cumin
- ½ teaspoon ground cinnamon
- ½ teaspoon garlic powder
- ⅛ teaspoon cayenne pepper, or to taste
- aluminum foil

Directions

- Step 1

Preheat the oven to 450 degrees F (230 degrees C).

- Step 2

Toss carrots in a bowl with olive oil, lemon juice, sugar, cumin, cinnamon, garlic powder, and cayenne pepper. Transfer to a large roasting pan and arrange in a single layer.

- Step 3

Roast in the preheated oven, often turning for 20 to 30 minutes.

Nutrition Facts

151 calories; protein 1.5g; carbohydrates 16.8g; fat 9.5g; sodium 105.3mg

Crispy Baked Moroccan Chicken Wings with Yogurt Dip

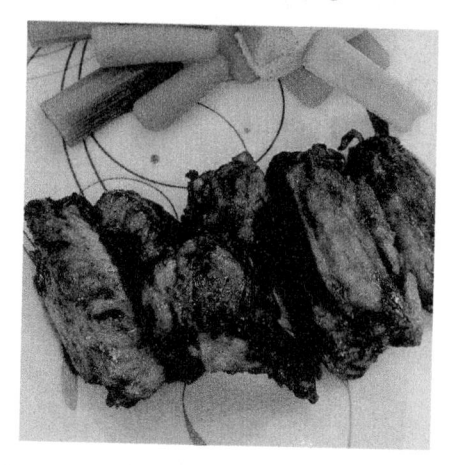

Ditch the deep fryer in favor of flavor-packed baked chicken wings coated in Moroccan spices and crisped to perfection atop a foil-lined baking sheet from Kelly Senyei of Just a Taste. Dunk the spiced wings in a refreshing herb yogurt dip made with mint, cilantro, lemon juice, and honey.

Prep time: 15 mins
Servings: 4 servings

∽

Ingredients

Chicken Wings:

- 2 ½ pounds chicken wings

- 1 ½ tablespoon of vegetable oil
- 1 teaspoon paprika
- 1 teaspoon ground cumin
- ¼ teaspoon ground cinnamon
- ¼ teaspoon ground ginger
- ¼ teaspoon cayenne pepper
- ¼ teaspoon ground turmeric
- ½ teaspoon salt
- ¼ teaspoon pepper
- Reynolds Wrap Non-Stick Aluminum Foil

Yogurt Dip:

- 1 cup plain Greek yogurt
- 2 tablespoons fresh lemon juice
- 1 tablespoon chopped fresh mint
- 1 tablespoon chopped fresh cilantro
- 1 ½ tablespoon of honey
- ½ teaspoon salt
- ¼ teaspoon pepper

Directions

- **Step 1**

Preheat the oven to 400 degrees F. Line a baking sheet with Reynolds Wrap Non-Stick Foil. Add the chicken wings to a large bowl, drizzle them with the vegetable oil, then toss until the wings are thoroughly coated.

- **Step 2**

In a small bowl, stir together the paprika, cumin, cinnamon, ginger, cayenne, turmeric, salt, and pepper. Sprinkle the wings with the spice mixture, tossing until they are coated. Arrange the wings in a single layer on the baking sheet, spacing them apart, so they aren't touching.

- Step 3

Bake the wings for 40 to 45 minutes until they are cooked through, then transfer them to a serving platter.

- Step 4

In a small bowl, stir together the yogurt, lemon juice, mint, cilantro, honey, salt, and pepper. Taste and season the dip with additional salt and pepper as desired. Serve the wings with the yogurt dip.

Notes

Line a baking sheet with Reynolds Wrap Heavy Duty Foil for quick and easy cleanup every time!

Nutrition Facts

347 calories; protein 22.3g; carbohydrates 10.3g; fat 24.1g; cholesterol 70.7mg; sodium 673.9mg.

Moroccan Semolina Soup with Milk, Anise Seeds, and Honey

This simple Moroccan soup is easy to prepare and can be served in the evening or as a breakfast porridge. Serve warm, garnished with cinnamon, with honey for sweetening on the side.

Prep time: 10 mins
Servings: 4 servings

Ingredients

- 4 cups water
- ¾ cup coarse semolina flour
- 1 ¼ teaspoons salt, or to taste
- 3 cups milk
- 2 tablespoons butter
- 1 teaspoon anise seed, or more to taste

Directions

- **Step 1**

Bring water to a boil in a saucepan and stir in semolina and salt. Simmer gently, frequently stirring, until the semolina is tender and mixture is very thick, 10 to 15 minutes. Stir in milk, butter, and anise seed; simmer until soup reaches desired consistency, 5 to 10 minutes.

- **Step 2**

Stir milk, butter, and anise seed into soup; simmer until soup reaches desired consistency, 5 to 10 minutes.

Notes

You can substitute fennel seeds for anise seeds if desired.
The soup will thicken as it cools. Stir in additional water to thin the soup when reheating.

Nutrition Facts

144 calories; protein 6.2g; carbohydrates 8.8g; fat 9.4g; cholesterol 29.9mg; sodium 849.8mg

Moroccan Sweet Potato and Raisin Salad

This sweet Moroccan salad is prepared by simmering diced sweet potatoes or yams with cinnamon, turmeric, saffron, raisins, and honey. It is an easy dish with an exotic taste.

Prep time: 15 mins
Servings: 4 servings

Ingredients

- ⅓ cup raisins
- 1 pound sweet potatoes, peeled and cut into 1/2-inch cubes
- 2 cups water
- 2 tablespoons honey
- 2 tablespoons butter
- ½ teaspoon salt
- ½ teaspoon ground cinnamon
- ¼ teaspoon ground black pepper

- ⅛ teaspoon ground turmeric
- 3 saffron threads, crumbled, or to taste

Directions

- **Step 1**

Place raisins into a bowl, cover with boiling water and let stand to plump.

- **Step 2**

Place sweet potatoes into a saucepan, cover with 2 cups water, and bring to a boil. Add honey, butter, salt, cinnamon, black pepper, turmeric, and saffron to potatoes; reduce heat to low. Simmer until potatoes are tender but not mushy, 8 to 10 minutes. Drain raisins and stir into sweet potato mixture.

- **Step 3**

Continue to simmer until the mixture has thickened, about 10 more minutes. Let cool before serving.

Nutrition Facts

218 calories; protein 2.3g; carbohydrates 41.4g; fat 5.9g; cholesterol 15.3mg; sodium 399.4mg.

Cucumber Raita

Serve this cool, refreshing salad with my Lamb Tagine and Moroccan Couscous on this site. Make the salad early in the day and keep it in the refrigerator to let the flavors blend and intensify. Add more mint to taste, but do not substitute dried mint; the flavor is just not the same.

Prep time: 15 mins
Servings: 12 servings

Ingredients

- 2 hot-house cucumber - peeled, seeded, and thinly sliced
- 2 cups Greek yogurt
- 3 tablespoons lemon juice

- 2 tablespoons chopped fresh mint
- ½ teaspoon white sugar
- ¼ teaspoon kosher salt

Directions

- Step 1

Stir together the cucumber, yogurt, lemon juice, mint, sugar, and salt in a bowl. Cover and refrigerate for at least 3 hours, preferably overnight.

Note

To make your own Greek yogurt, place 2 1/2 cups of plain, nonfat yogurt in a strainer lined with several layers of cheesecloth. Place over a bowl, cover, and refrigerate overnight. Discard the liquid collected in the bowl, and proceed with the recipe!

Nutrition Facts

50 calories; protein 2.5g; carbohydrates 2.8g; fat 3.3g; cholesterol 7.5mg; sodium 61.7mg.

Moroccan Lamb with Shiraz Honey Sauce

A delicious Moroccan-inspired rack of lamb. Serve with honey-glazed carrots and rosemary mashed potatoes. Ras el hanout is a traditional and complex Moroccan spice blend and may be found in specialty grocery stores.

Prep time: 20 mins
Servings: 4 servings

Ingredients

- 1 (7 bone) rack of lamb, trimmed and frenched
- coarse sea salt to taste
- 2 ½ tablespoons ras el hanout
- 1 cup Shiraz wine
- ⅓ cup honey

Directions

- **Step 1**

Preheat oven to 400 degrees F (200 degrees C).

- **Step 2**

Season lamb with sea salt, and rub with ras el hanout. In a medium cast-iron skillet over medium-high heat, sear lamb on all sides until evenly browned.

- **Step 3**

Place skillet with lamb in the preheated oven, roast for 30 minutes, or until the internal temperature has reached a minimum of 145 degrees F (63 degrees C).

- **Step 4**

Remove lamb from skillet, reserve juices, and rest 10 to 15 minutes before slicing ribs. Place skillet with juices over medium heat, and stir in wine and honey. Cook until reduced by about half. Drizzle over ribs to serve.

Nutrition Facts

907 calories; protein 35g; carbohydrates 26.6g; fat 69.3g; cholesterol 165.8mg; sodium 136mg.

Vegetable Tagine

A flavorful and delicious meal. A must-try!

Prep time: 25 mins
Servings: 6 servings

Ingredients

- 1 tablespoon olive oil
- 1 onion, chopped
- 1 green bell pepper, chopped
- 3 cloves garlic, chopped
- 3 carrots, chopped
- 2 sweet potatoes, chopped
- 1 eggplant, chopped
- 4 plum tomatoes, chopped

- 3 zucchini, chopped
- ½ cup raisins
- 3 (16 ounces) of cans chicken broth
- 2 tablespoons lemon juice
- 1 tablespoon honey
- ¼ teaspoon ground cumin
- ¼ teaspoon ground coriander
- ¼ teaspoon ground turmeric
- ¼ teaspoon ground cinnamon
- 1 (15.5 ounces) of can garbanzo beans, rinsed and drained
- 1 teaspoon salt
- 1 teaspoon ground black pepper

Directions

- Step 1

Heat oil in the bottom of a large, heavy pot over medium-high heat. Cook and stir the onion, green bell pepper, and garlic in the oil until tender, about 5 minutes.

- Step 2

Place the carrots, sweet potatoes, eggplant, plum tomatoes, zucchini, and raisins in the pot with the onion mixture. Stir in the chicken broth, lemon juice, honey, and season with cumin, coriander, turmeric, and cinnamon. Bring the stew to a boil over high heat, cover, reduce the heat to medium-low, and simmer until the vegetables are tender about 30 minutes.

- Step 3

Pour the garbanzo beans into the stew and season with salt and pepper. Stir to combine and cook the soup for an additional 10 to 15 minutes.

Nutrition Facts

---

282 calories; protein 9.1g; carbohydrates 55.6g; fat 4.3g; cholesterol 5.7mg; sodium 1774.1mg.

Moroccan Tagine of Shrimp in Tomato Sauce

A zesty homemade tomato sauce with Moroccan spices forms the base for this flavorful shrimp tagine.

Note that we like to remove the tails from the shrimp for ease of eating; you may leave the tails on if you prefer. Note also that the prep time will be reduced if you are using shrimp that has already been shelled and cleaned.

Cooking directions call for preparing the sauce and shrimp in a traditional Moroccan tagine. If you don't have one, you may use a deep skillet instead, or you might like to try cooking in a tagra, which can be covered loosely with aluminum foil.

Prep time: 45 minutes

Servings: 4-6 servings

Ingredients

- 2 pounds 3 ounces/1 kilogram shrimp (large)
- 2 pounds 3 ounces/1 kilogram tomatoes (fresh and ripe)
- 1/3 cup olive oil
- 1 medium onion (finely chopped)
- 7 cloves of garlic (pressed)
- 1 1/2 teaspoon paprika
- 1 1/2 teaspoon cumin
- 1 1/2 teaspoon salt (or to taste)
- 1/2 teaspoon ginger
- 1/2 teaspoon cayenne pepper
- 2 tablespoons fresh parsley (finely chopped)
- 2 tablespoons fresh coriander (finely chopped)
- Optional: 1 bay leaf
- Garnish: parsley (chopped fresh)
- Garnish: black pepper (coarsely ground)
- Garnish: lemon (slices or wedges)

Directions

Clean the Shrimp

- Gather the ingredients.
- Wash the shrimp under running water and drain.
- Remove the head, legs, and shells (and tails if desired)

- Devein the shrimp if necessary.
- Wash the shrimp again and set it aside in a colander to drain.

<u>**Make the Tomato Sauce**</u>

- Gather the ingredients.
- Peel, seed, and chop the tomatoes. (Or, if the tomatoes are very soft, you can cut them in half, seed them and grate them.)
- Set the tomatoes aside.
- Place the base of a large tagine over medium-low heat. (The use of a diffuser between the heat source and tagine is recommended.)
- Add the olive oil and onions and saute gently for several minutes or until the onions begin to soften.
- Add the garlic and saute just for a minute or two, until very fragrant.
- Remember to maintain low heat and avoid burning the garlic.
- Add the tomatoes, spices, and herbs and stir to combine.
- Cover, and allow the tagine to reach a simmer slowly.
- Do not increase the heat to speed things up.
- Continue simmering the tomatoes, occasionally stirring, for about 30 minutes, or until the tomatoes can be mashed with the back of a spoon and a thick sauce forms.

<u>**Cook the Shrimp**</u>

- Add the cleaned shrimp to the tomato sauce, along

- with a few tablespoons of water if you feel the sauce should be thinned, and cover.
- Cook the shrimp for several minutes, then stir gently to turn the shrimp over.
- Continue cooking for several minutes more until the shrimp are just done.
- Remove the tagine from the heat.

<u>*To Serve*</u>

- When ready to serve, discard the bay leaf and garnish the tagine with chopped parsley, a few turns of the pepper mill, and fresh lemon slices. Wedges of lemon may be offered on the side.
- It is customary to serve the shrimp directly from the tagine, with each person eating from his side of the dish. Instead of a fork, Moroccan bread is used to scoop up the shrimp and sauce.
- Enjoy!

Nutrition Facts

Calories: 380; Fat: 15g; Saturated Fat: 2g; Cholesterol: 333mg; Sodium: 1481mg; Carbohydrate: 23g; Dietary Fiber: 4g; Protein: 43g; Calcium: 228mg

Moroccan Berber Tagine With Lamb or Beef and Vegetables

Moroccan tagines that combine meat and vegetables make wonderful one-dish meals to offer at family dinners or when entertaining casually. They can be slow-cooked on the stove or prepped indoors and then cooked outside over charcoal for backyard dining or beach outings and picnics.

Berber style tagines such as this one are distinguished not only by the seasoning but also by the presentation of ingredients. The vegetables are carefully arranged in conical fashion around the beef or lamb, fully concealing the meat in an artistic, appetizing manner.

Although many of the tagine recipes on this site include directions for alternative preparations in a pot or pressure cooker, this one is best slow-cooked in the traditional clay or ceramic vessel from which it takes its name. The seasoning below is ideal when using potatoes as the dominant ingredient, but other vegetables are added for color and complementary flavor. Here I'm recommending carrots and zucchini, but either or both can be replaced with fresh peas, green beans, sliced tomatoes, turnips, or other veggies you might have on hand.

Preserved lemon and olives are classic additions and add a distinctive flavor and some saltiness, but they may be omitted if you don't have them on hand. Adjust salt accordingly. If using chicken instead of red meat, see the tips below.

The tagine serves as both the cooking vessel and serving dish; diners gather around and eat from their side of the tagine using Moroccan bread (khobz) in place of a utensil.

Prep time: 25 minutes
Servings: 4 servings

Ingredients

- 1 pound beef (or lamb, cut into 2" to 3" pieces)
- 1/4 to 1/3 cup olive oil
- 1 medium onion (sliced)
- 1 medium onion (finely chopped)
- 3 to 4 cloves garlic (finely chopped or pressed)
- 3 to 4 small potatoes (or medium, quartered lengthwise)
- 3 to 4 medium carrots (halved or quartered lengthwise)
- Optional: 4 small zucchini (whole; or may use other veggies)
- 1 small bell pepper (any color, cut into strips or rings)
- 1 small handful of parsley (and/or cilantro, tied into a bouquet)
- Optional: 1 small jalapeno or chili pepper
- 1 small preserved lemon (quartered)
- 1 handful olives (green or red/violet)

For the Seasoning:

- 1 teaspoon salt (or to taste)
- 1 teaspoon ginger
- 1/2 teaspoon black pepper
- 1/2 teaspoon turmeric
- 1/2 teaspoon paprika
- 1/2 teaspoon cumin
- Optional: 1/4 teaspoon cayenne pepper
- Optional: 1 pinch saffron threads

Directions

- Pour the olive oil into the base of a tagine.
- Arrange the onion rings across the bottom and scatter the chopped onion and garlic on top.
- Arrange the meat, bone-side down, in a mound in the center of the tagine. (The taller the mound, the more conical your arrangement of vegetables will be.)
- Combine the spices in a small bowl.
- Sprinkle a little less than half of the seasoning over the meat and onions.
- Place the prepped vegetables in a large bowl.
- Add the remaining seasoning and toss to coat the vegetables evenly.
- Arrange the vegetables in a conical shape around the meat.
- Arrange the bell pepper strips in the center and top with the parsley bouquet and then the jalapeno pepper; garnish the tagine with the preserved lemon quarters and olives.

- Add 2 1/2 cups water to the empty bowl and swirl to rinse the residual spices.
- Add the water to the tagine, cover, and place the tagine over medium coals in a brazier or stovetop over medium-low heat. Using a diffuser under the tagine is necessary if using clay or ceramic on an electric stove and recommended for other heat sources.
- Leave the tagine to reach a simmer. This may take a long time, 20 minutes or so; be cautious in feeling the need to increase the heat.
- Once simmering, continue cooking the tagine over medium-low heat until the meat and vegetables are very tender, and the sauce is reduced, up to 3 hours for beef and up to 4 hours for lamb.
- While the tagine is cooking, you may check the level of the liquids occasionally and add a little water as necessary, but otherwise, try not to disturb the tagine.
- Do stay alert for the smell of anything burning, and lower the heat if necessary to avoid scorching ingredients and/or cracking the tagine. However, it is normal for some of the base onions to burn and adhere to the bottom of the tagine as they caramelize and reduce.
- Remove the cooked tagine from the heat and serve. It will stay warm while covered for 30 minutes.

Note

If you want to use chicken in place of lamb or beef, you may leave the skin on or remove it; arrange the chicken meat-side (or skin-side) up. Cooking directions will remain the same, except that you should reduce the water to 1 1/2 cups and reduce the cooking time to 2 hours, or until the veggies test is done. To compensate for the shorter cooking time, it may be helpful to use smaller potatoes and carrots and briefly parboil legumes such as peas and green beans before adding them to the tagine.

Nutrition Facts

Calories: 673; Fat: 39g; Saturated Fat: 12g; Cholesterol: 106mg; Sodium: 747mg; Carbohydrate: 50g; Dietary Fiber: 9g; Protein 35g; Calcium 169mg.

Vegetable Curry Couscous

A variety of veggies make this interesting side dish versatile. You can serve chicken in an apple, onion, and curry sauce over the top and sprinkle it with flaked coconut. It can also be made with quinoa; just adjust the cooking time.

Prep time: 30 mins
Servings: 4 servings

∼

Ingredients

- 1 teaspoon vegetable oil
- ½ small onion, chopped
- 1 small leek, cleaned and thinly sliced
- 1 stalk celery, thinly sliced
- ½ red bell pepper, chopped
- 3 cloves garlic, minced
- 1 ½ cups chicken stock
- 1 carrot, grated
- 2 tomatoes - peeled, seeded, and chopped
- ½ cup couscous
- ¼ cup golden raisins
- ¼ cup dried currants
- 1 teaspoon curry powder, or to taste
- 1 pinch ground turmeric, or to taste
- salt and ground black pepper to taste
- 2 tablespoons sliced almonds

Directions

- **Step 1**

Place vegetable oil in a saucepan over medium heat, cook, and stir the onion, leek, celery, red bell pepper, and garlic until the onion is translucent for about 5 minutes.

- **Step 2**

Pour in the chicken stock, bring to a boil, and stir in the carrot, tomatoes, couscous, raisins, and currants. Season with curry powder, turmeric, salt, and black pepper; bring the mixture back to a boil. Reduce heat to low, cover the pan, and allow to cook for 5 minutes.

- **Step 3**

Remove from heat. Let the couscous stand covered for 5 minutes, and fluff with a fork. Sprinkle with sliced almonds.

Notes

Please add curry in half-teaspoon increments to achieve desired flavor and heat. Most couscous will cook in five minutes.

Nutrition Facts

209 calories; protein 5.8g; carbohydrates 41.3g; fat 3.5g; cholesterol 0.3mg; sodium 288.3mg.

Moroccan Sausage and Egg Tagine

Sausage and eggs are Moroccan comfort food, quickly prepared by cooking sausage and adding eggs to the pan. This simple dish becomes a hearty and flavorful meal by adding caramelizing onions and adding tomatoes, olives, and meat.

Moroccans often serve egg dishes directly from the pan in which they're cooked, using crusty Moroccan bread instead of a fork. For a zesty variation, use Moroccan Merguez sausage with your and eggs and tomatoes.

Prep time: 10 minutes
Servings: 4 servings

∼

Ingredients

- 8 ounces/225 grams merguez (or similar sausage)
- 1 large onion (finely chopped)
- 2 medium tomatoes (peeled, seeded, and chopped)
- A handful of olives (green, pitted, sliced)
- 1/2 teaspoon salt
- 1/2 teaspoon cumin
- 1/4 teaspoon black pepper (or 1/8 teaspoon cayenne pepper)
- A small handful of chopped cilantro (or parsley)
- 6 large eggs
- Salt (to taste)
- Cumin (to taste)
- Garnish: cilantro (chopped or parsley)

Directions

- Gather the ingredients.
- Cook the sausage in a large skillet or the base of a tagine until the meat tests as done. (If there is a large amount of fat from the sausage, remove the excess, leaving enough to continue cooking. If the sausage was low-fat, you might need to add a little olive oil to the pan at this point.)
- Add the onion, tomatoes, olives, and seasoning and cook for about 5 minutes.
- Pour the eggs directly over the sausage and veggies.
- Break the yolks, and allow the eggs to simmer until set. (To help this along, you can lift the edges of the eggs as they cook and tip the pan to allow uncooked egg to run underneath and cook faster.)
- If cooking the eggs in a tagine, cover the eggs and allow them to poach until done.

- Dust the top of the cooked eggs with cumin and salt to taste, garnish with a little chopped parsley, and serve.
- Enjoy

Nutrition Facts

Calories: 252; Fat: 18g; Saturated Fat: 6g; Cholesterol: 257mg; Sodium: 556mg; Carbohydrate 8g; Dietary Fiber 1g; Protein 15g; Calcium 66mg

---

Moroccan Chicken and Apricot Tagine

Dried or fresh fruits are often key additions to sweet and savory Moroccan tagines such as this one. Here, chicken is stewed until tender with onions, saffron, ginger, and pepper, and the dish is then topped with apricots and a honey-cinnamon syrup. Fried almonds or sesame seeds are traditional but optional garnishes.

The seasoning here reflects a preference for fruit tagines that are zesty and a bit peppery. Feel free to reduce the white and black peppers (and Ras el Hanout) if you want a mild side season. Keep in mind that the cooking time is for traditional clay or ceramic tagine preparation. If you prepare this dish with conventional cookware, the ingredients will cook faster, so keep an eye on the chicken and sauce to make sure it doesn't overcook; you may need to reduce the cooking time by up to an hour.

Prep time: *15 minutes*
Servings: *4 servings*

~

Ingredients

<u>**For the Chicken:**</u>

- 1 whole chicken (cut into 4 or 8 pieces)
- 3/4 teaspoon salt
- 1 1/4 teaspoons freshly grated ginger
- 1/2 teaspoon saffron threads (crumbled)
- 1/2 teaspoon black pepper
- 1/4 teaspoon white pepper
- 1/4 teaspoon Ras el Hanout, optional
- 1/2 teaspoon turmeric

<u>**For the Tagine:**</u>

- 3 tablespoons butter
- 2 tablespoons olive oil
- 2 medium onions (grated)
- 3 to 4 cloves garlic (pressed or finely chopped)
- 1 or 2 small pieces of cinnamon stick (about 3 inches)
- A small handful of cilantro sprigs tied into a bouquet

- 1/2 cup chicken broth
- 3/4 cup water
- 3 tablespoons sugar or honey
- 1 cup dried apricots
- 1 teaspoon ground cinnamon
- A handful of fried almonds, optional
- 1 to 2 teaspoons sesame seeds, optional

Directions

- Gather the chicken ingredients.
- Combine the spices in a bowl large enough to hold the chicken.
- Add the chicken and toss to coat the pieces with the spices evenly.
- Gather the remaining tagine ingredients.
- Over medium-low heat, melt the butter in the base of a large tagine or Dutch oven.
- Add the olive oil, onions, garlic, and cinnamon stick.
- Add the seasoned chicken, meat-side down, in a single layer on top of the onions.
- Place the cilantro bouquet on top. Add the broth to the tagine.
- In the bowl used to season the chicken, swirl the water to cleanse it of the spices.
- Add the water to the tagine.
- Cover and leave the liquids to reach a simmer over medium-low heat.
- Once simmering, cook the chicken, undisturbed, for 1 hour.
- Remove 1/2 cup of the cooking liquids and set aside.
- Carefully turn over the chicken pieces so that they are

meat-side up.
- Cover the pan and continue simmering for another 30 minutes to 1 hour, until the chicken is done and the liquids are thick and reduced.
- While the chicken is cooking, put the apricots in a small pot and cover them with water.
- Simmer the apricots over medium heat, partially covered, for 10 to 15 minutes, or until tender enough to pinch in half with your fingers.
- Drain the apricots and return to the pot.
- Add the sugar (or honey), ground cinnamon, and 1/2 cup of the reserved cooking liquid.
- Simmer the apricots gently for 5 to 10 minutes, or until they are sitting in a thick syrup.
- Discard the cilantro bouquet and cinnamon stick from the tagine.
- Arrange the chicken on a large serving platter (or leave it in the base of the tagine). Spoon the apricots and syrup on and around the chicken. If desired, garnish with fried almonds or sesame seeds.

Nutrition Facts

Calories: 688; Fat: 39g; Saturated Fat: 13g; Cholesterol: 175mg; Sodium: 766mg; Carbohydrate: 38g; Dietary Fiber: 4g; Sugars: 29g; Protein: 48g; Vitamin C: 4mg; Calcium: 81mg; Iron: 4mg; Potassium: 880mg.

Moroccan Tagine with Olives and Artichoke Hearts

A delicious Moroccan stew that can be served over couscous or saffron rice. This dish can also be made vegetarian by omitting the chicken.

Prep time: 15 mins
Servings: 6 servings

Ingredients

- 1 tablespoon olive oil
- 2 skinless, boneless chicken breast halves - cut into chunks
- ½ onion, chopped
- 3 cloves garlic, minced
- 1 (15.5 ounces) of can garbanzo beans, drained and rinsed
- 1 (14.5 ounces) of can diced tomatoes with juice
- 1 (14 ounces) of can vegetable broth
- 1 (14 ounces) of can quartered artichoke hearts, drained

- 1 carrot, peeled and chopped
- ½ cup sliced Mediterranean black olives
- 1 tablespoon white sugar
- 1 tablespoon lemon juice
- 1 teaspoon salt
- 1 teaspoon ground coriander
- 1 pinch cayenne pepper

Directions

- **Step 1**

Heat olive oil in a large skillet over medium heat. Cook and stir chicken, onion, and garlic in hot oil until the chicken is no longer pink in the center, about 15 minutes.

- **Step 2**

Stir garbanzo beans, diced tomatoes with juice, vegetable broth, artichoke hearts, carrot, olives, sugar, lemon juice, salt, coriander, and cayenne pepper into the chicken mixture; bring to a boil, reduce heat to low, and simmer until vegetables are tender for about 30 minutes.

Nutrition Facts

229 calories; protein 14.1g; carbohydrates 31.2g; fat 5.4g; cholesterol 20.3mg; sodium 1219.7mg

One-Pot Moroccan Shrimp Tagine

The rich, exotic flavors of Morocco shine through in this delicious, one-pot shrimp tagine dish! Serve over prepared couscous.

Prep time: 20 minutes
Servings: 6 servings

∼

Ingredients

- 3 tablespoons olive oil
- 4 large carrots, chopped
- 1 large sweet onion, diced
- 1 large russet potato, peeled and diced
- 1 red bell pepper, thinly sliced
- ½ cup pitted Kalamata olives, sliced
- 2 tablespoons minced garlic
- 2 teaspoons ginger paste
- 2 large tomatoes, coarsely chopped

- ½ cup chopped fresh cilantro
- 1 tablespoon dried parsley
- 2 teaspoons ground cumin
- 2 teaspoons seasoned salt
- 1 (1.41 ounce) package sazon seasoning with saffron (such as Goya® Azafran)
- 1 teaspoon paprika
- 1 teaspoon ground turmeric
- 1 teaspoon lemon juice
- ½ teaspoon cayenne pepper
- ½ teaspoon ground black pepper
- 1 bay leaf
- 1 pound uncooked medium shrimp, peeled and deveined

Directions

- **Step 1**

Heat a Dutch oven over medium-high heat. Add olive oil. Saute carrots, onion, potato, and bell pepper until soft, about 5 minutes. Add olives, garlic, and ginger paste and saute for 2 minutes.

- **Step 2**

Stir in tomatoes, cilantro, parsley, cumin, seasoned salt, sazon, paprika, turmeric, lemon juice, cayenne, black pepper, and bay leaf. Cover and cook until tomatoes have broken down and flavors have combined for about 20 minutes. Add shrimp, cover, and cook until they are bright pink, about 5 minutes.

Nutrition Facts

---

275 calories; protein 16.3g; carbohydrates 28.8g; fat 11.2g; cholesterol 115mg; sodium 1669.8mg

---

Moroccan Kefta Tagine

A favorite of children and adults alike, kefta mkaouara (or Mmawra) presents petite, cherry-sized meatballs in a zesty homemade tomato sauce. Traditionally this famous Moroccan dish is prepared in a tagine, which lends earthy flavor, but a deep, wide skillet or Dutch oven will work just fine. Eggs are often added to the dish at the end of cooking; they're allowed to poach just until the whites set.

The well-seasoned meatballs are easy to make, but a set of extra hands will make shorter work of this step. Plan to start simmering the sauce while you shape with the kefta, which can be made from ground lamb, ground beef, or a combination of the two. An egg is not traditionally used as a binder, but if your meat is extra lean, go ahead and use one. Likewise, breadcrumbs are not normally used as a filler, but if you prefer a softer, spongier texture to your meatballs, a half cup or so may be added.

The final presentation is comfort food that begs you to dip right on in with crusty Moroccan bread. Kefta mkaouara is traditionally served from the same dish in which it was prepared, with each person using bread for scooping up the meatballs from his own side of the dish.

Prep time: 30 minutes
Servings: 4 servings

Ingredients

For the Tomato Sauce:

- 2 pounds tomatoes (fresh, ripe)
- Optional: 1 medium onion (finely chopped)
- 1/3 cup olive oil
- 3 tablespoons fresh parsley (chopped)
- 3 tablespoons fresh cilantro (chopped)
- 3 to 5 cloves garlic (pressed)
- 1 1/2 teaspoons paprika
- 1 1/2 teaspoons cumin
- 1 1/2 teaspoons salt
- 1/4 teaspoon black pepper
- 1 bay leaf

For the Kefta Meatballs:

- 1 pound ground beef (or lamb, or a combination of the two)
- 1 medium onion (chopped very fine)
- 1 small green pepper (finely chopped)
- 1/4 cup fresh parsley (chopped, plus more for garnish)
- 1/4 cup fresh cilantro (chopped, plus more for garnish)
- 1 to 2 teaspoons paprika
- 1 teaspoon cumin
- 1 teaspoon salt
- 1/2 teaspoon ground cinnamon
- 1/4 teaspoon black pepper
- 1/4 to 1/8 teaspoon cayenne pepper
- Optional: 1 or 2 chili peppers
- 1/4 cup water
- 3 or 4 eggs

Directions

While there are multiple steps to this recipe, this kefta dish is broken down into workable categories to help you better plan for preparation and cooking.

Prepare the Tomato Sauce:

- Gather the ingredients.
- Peel, seed, chop the tomatoes, or if they're very ripe, cut the tomatoes in half, seed them, and grate them.
- Mix the tomatoes with 1 finely chopped medium onion (if using), olive oil, parsley, cilantro, garlic, paprika, cumin, salt, black pepper, and bay leaf in the base of a tagine or a large, deep skillet.
- Cover and bring to a simmer over medium-low to medium heat. (Note: If using clay or ceramic tagine on

a heat source other than gas, be sure to place a diffuser between the tagine and burner.)
- Once simmering, reduce the heat a bit and allow the sauce to simmer gently, at least 15 to 20 minutes but longer if you like, before adding the meatballs.

__Make the Kefta Meatballs:__

- Gather the ingredients.
- Combine the ground beef or lamb, onion, green pepper, parsley, cilantro, paprika, cumin, salt, cinnamon, black pepper, and cayenne pepper.
- Using your hands to knead in the spices and herbs, shape the kefta mixture into very small meatballs the size of large cherries—about 3/4-inch in diameter.
- Add the meatballs (and chili peppers, if using) to the tomato sauce, along with a little water—1/4 cup is usually sufficient—and cover.
- Cook for about 30 to 40 minutes, or until the sauce is thick.
- Add the eggs to the tagine without breaking the yolks.
- Cover and cook for an additional 7 to 10 minutes, or until the egg whites are solid and the yolks are only partially set.
- If desired, garnish with fresh parsley or cilantro, and serve immediately. Enjoy!

Nutrition Facts

Calories: 712; Fat: 47g; Saturated Fat: 14g; Cholesterol: 315mg; Sodium: 1747mg; Carbohydrate: 34g; Dietary Fiber: 8g; Protein: 42g; Calcium: 224mg

---

Pressure Cooker Moroccan Lamb or Beef Tagine With Prunes

Beef or lamb with prunes is a classic sweet and savory Moroccan dish that combines dried prunes and meat with the fragrant spices of ginger, saffron, cinnamon, and pepper. It's popular as a traditional offering at holiday gatherings, weddings, and other special occasions.

Of course, no special occasion is needed for a tagine of lamb with prunes to appear on the table. Prep work is minimal, making it a perfect choice for casual family meals. Although a Moroccan clay or ceramic tagine is most traditional, most Moroccan cooks prepare this dish in a pressure cooker as it speeds things up. Tender cuts of meat (some pieces on the bone) will give the best results.

The cooking time listed below is for the pressure cooker method. Double or triple this time if using a conventional pot or tagine. Note that the onion preparation is different from the tagine method.

Prep time: *15 minutes*
Servings: *4-6 servings*

∼

Ingredients

- 2 pounds tender beef or lamb, cut into 3-inch pieces
- 2 medium onions, grated or very finely chopped
- 3 cloves garlic, finely chopped or pressed
- 3/4 teaspoon salt
- 1 teaspoon ground black pepper
- 1 teaspoon ground ginger
- 1/2 teaspoon saffron threads, crumbled
- 1/2 teaspoon turmeric
- 1 to 2 (3- to 4-inch) pieces cinnamon stick
- 1/4 cup olive oil
- 1/4 cup butter, softened
- 2 1/2 cups water
- A handful of cilantro sprigs tied together
- 1/2 pound prunes
- 1 tablespoon honey
- 2 tablespoons sugar
- 1 1/2 teaspoons ground cinnamon
- Optional: 1 tablespoon toasted sesame seeds
- Optional: Handful of fried almonds

Directions

While there are multiple steps to this recipe, this Moroccan dish is broken down into workable categories to help you better plan for preparation and cooking.

Cook the Meat:

- Gather the ingredients.
- In a bowl, mix the meat with onions, garlic, and spices.
- Heat the oil and butter in a skillet over medium heat and brown the meat for a few minutes until a crust forms.
- Place the meat mixture in the pressure cooker and add 2 1/2 cups of water and the cilantro. Over high heat, bring the meat and liquids to a simmer.
- Cover tightly and continue heating until pressure is achieved. Reduce the heat to medium, and cook with pressure for 45 to 50 minutes.
- About halfway through cooking, remove 1/2 cup of the liquid and reserve.
- After the meat has cooked, release the pressure and reduce the sauce, uncovered, until it is mostly oil and onion.

Cook the Prunes:

- While the meat is cooking, put the prunes in a small pot and cover them with water. Simmer over medium heat, partially covered, until the prunes are tender enough to pinch off the pit or pinch in half easily. (The amount of time this takes can vary greatly depending on the prunes, but the average is 15 to 30 minutes.)
- Drain the prunes, then add 1/2 cup of the reserved liquid from the meat.
- Stir in the honey, sugar, and ground cinnamon, and

simmer the prunes for another 5 to 10 minutes, or until they are sitting in a thick syrup.

To Serve:

- Arrange the meat on a large serving platter and spoon the prunes and syrup on top.
- If desired, garnish with sesame seeds and/or fried almonds. Moroccan tradition gathers around the table and eats from this communal plate, using Moroccan bread to scoop up the meat and sauce.

Nutrition Facts

Calories: 753; Total Fat: 48g; Saturated Fat: 19g; Cholesterol: 162mg; Sodium: 124mg; Carbohydrate: 43g; Dietary Fiber: 4g; Protein: 40g; Calcium: 117mg.

Moroccan Tagine with Fish and Rice

Moroccan Tagine with Fish and Rice recipe is a flavorful and easy one-pot meal that cooks fish and rice together with traditional Moroccan ingredients.

Prep time: 10 minutes
Servings: 1 serving

Ingredients

- 3 tablespoons olive oil
- 1 cup chopped onion

- 4-5 cloves garlic minced
- ½ cup chopped cilantro
- 2 tablespoons fresh grated ginger
- 2 teaspoons ground cumin
- 1 teaspoon ground coriander
- 1 teaspoon ground cinnamon
- 1 ½ cups basmati rice or long grain
- 15 ounce can diced tomatoes
- 15 ounce can chickpeas drained
- 6 ounce pitted green olives drained
- ¾ cup golden raisins
- ½ cup dried apricots halved
- 1 lemon zested and juiced
- 4-6 thin white fish fillets: flounder, grouper, or snapper (optional)
- salt and pepper

Garnishes:

- ½ cup toasted almonds
- ½ cup fresh chopped mint
- ¼ cup cilantro
- pickled red onion (optional)

Directions

- Set a large Moroccan Tagine over low heat. (You could also use a large sauté pan with a tight lid.) Add the oil, onions, cilantro, garlic, and ginger. Sauté for 5-8 minutes.
- Then mix in the cumin, coriander, cinnamon, and rice. Stir and toast the spices and rice for another 2 minutes.

- Add the diced tomatoes, chickpeas, raisins, apricots, lemon zest and juice, and 1 ½ teaspoon salt to the rice. Mix well and spread evenly across the bottom of the pan. Then pour 1 ½ cups water over the top.
- Place the cover over the tagine and cook for 15-20 minutes. Do not lift the lid until the 15 minutes mark. The rice should look dry on top, and there should be a vent hole apparent. If it does not look fully cooked, cover and continue cooking for 5 more minutes.
- Adding Fish: If you plan to add fish at the end, pat the fish fillets dry. Then salt and pepper them liberally on both sides.
- Once the rice has cooked for at least 15 minutes, lay the fish fillets over the top of the rice and cover. You can either turn off the heat and let them steam for 5-10 minutes or if needed, you can continue cooking the rice for another 5 minutes, then turn off the heat. Either way, fish fillets under ½ inch thick will cook through on top of the rice in 5-10 minutes.
- Then remove the lid and sprinkle the top with fresh chopped mint, cilantro, and toasted almonds. Serve warm.

Notes

If you skip the fish, this is a vegan and plant-based recipe. With or without the fish, it is gluten-free and dairy-free.

Nutrition Facts

Calories: 578kcal, carbohydrates: 91g, protein: 15g, fat: 20g, saturated fat: 2g, sodium: 559mg, potassium: 871mg, fiber: 12g, sugar: 24g, vitamin a: 907iu, vitamin c: 22mg, calcium: 167mg, iron: 5mg.

Moroccan Vegetarian Carrot and Chickpea Tagine

Tagines are usually the main dish in Morocco, but this vegetarian version works equally well as a side to meat or poultry.

Chickpeas and carrots are stewed with piquant, aromatic seasonings including ginger, cinnamon, and the multi-spice know as ras el hanout. A touch of honey adds complementary sweetness.

When a recipe calls for chickpeas, the vast majority of Moroccans prefer to start with dried chickpeas rather than canned. If you want to follow suit, allow additional time to soak the chickpeas overnight, then cook until tender. This may be done well in advance, as it's perfectly fine to freeze cooked chickpeas until needed.

You have plenty of flexibility as to how to season the tagine. To add heat, throw in one or two chile peppers. For a sweeter presentation, increase the honey and include the optional raisins. Using half broth instead of all water will add depth of flavor, but be sure to watch the salt.

Although tagines are typically served with Moroccan bread for scooping everything up like a dip, you can break tradition and serve the chickpeas and carrots over a bed of rice or couscous.

Prep time: 15 minutes

Servings: 3-4 servings

Ingredients

- 1 large onion (chopped)
- 4 cloves garlic (finely chopped or pressed)
- 3 tablespoons olive oil
- 1 1/4 teaspoons salt, or to taste
- 1 teaspoon ginger
- 1 teaspoon turmeric
- 3/4 teaspoon cinnamon
- 1/2 teaspoon black pepper
- 1/4 teaspoon cayenne pepper
- Optional: 1/8 teaspoon Ras el hanout (or more to taste)
- 2 or 3 tablespoons chopped parsley or cilantro
- 4 or 5 peeled carrots (cut into 1/4-inch thick sticks)
- 1 cup water (half vegetable or chicken broth, if desired)
- 2 to 3 teaspoons honey (or to taste)
- 1 to 2 cups cooked or canned chickpeas (drained)

- Optional: 1 or 2 small chile peppers
- Optional: 1/4 cup golden raisins
- Garnish Optional: Additional parsley or cilantro

Directions

- Gather the ingredients.
- In the base of a tagine or a large skillet with a lid, sauté the onions and garlic in the olive oil over medium-low heat for several minutes.
- Add the salt, ginger, turmeric, cinnamon, black pepper, cayenne pepper, ras el hanout, parsley or cilantro, carrots, and the water.
- Bring to a simmer over medium-low heat, then continue cooking, covered, until the carrots are nearly cooked to desired tenderness. In a skillet, this may take up to 25 minutes, in a tagine a bit longer.
- Stir in the honey and add the chickpeas and optional chile peppers and raisins. Continue simmering until the chickpeas are heated through, and the sauce is reduced and thick.
- Taste, adjust seasoning if desired, and serve garnished with parsley or cilantro.
- Enjoy!

Nutrition Facts

Calories: 454; Fat: 14g; Saturated Fat: 2g; Cholesterol: 0mg; Sodium: 1280mg; Carbohydrate: 72g; Dietary Fiber: 14g; Protein 16g; Calcium 188mg.

Moroccan Lentil Soup with Veggies

Warm, intoxicating spices make this vegetable-filled Moroccan Lentil and Vegetable Stew perfect for cold Autumn nights.

Prep time: 5 mins
Servings: 8 servings

~

Ingredients

- 2 Tbsp olive oil
- 1 yellow onion

- 4 cloves garlic, minced
- 4 ribs celery
- 1/2 Tbsp ground cumin
- 1 tsp turmeric
- 1 tsp cinnamon
- 1/4 tsp cayenne pepper
- 1 15oz. can chickpeas
- 1 28oz. can diced tomatoes
- 1/2 lb. frozen cauliflower florets
- 6 cups vegetable broth
- 1 cup brown lentils
- 1 bay leaf

Directions

- Dice the onion and mince the garlic. Sauté both in a large pot with olive oil over medium heat until softened. Dice the celery while the onions and garlic are sautéing, add to the pot, and continue to sauté for 2-3 minutes more.
- Add the cumin, turmeric, cinnamon, and cayenne pepper to the pot. Stir and cook the spices with the vegetables for 1-2 minutes.
- Add the diced tomatoes (with juices), chickpeas (rinsed and drained), and cauliflower florets (no need to thaw). Stir the pot until everything is well mixed.
- Add the vegetable broth and bay leaf, turn the heat up to high, place a lid on the pot, and allow it to come to a boil. Once it reaches a boil, add the lentils. Stir and let it come back up to a boil, then turn the heat down to low. Let the stew simmer on low, with the lid, for 30 minutes.

- After simmering for 30 minutes, the lentils should be tender. Remove the bay leaf and give the stew a taste. Add salt if needed (this will depend on the type of vegetable broth used. I did not add any additional salt), then serve.

Nutrition Facts

Calories: 238.79kcal, Carbohydrates: 37.84g, Protein: 12.2g, Fat: 5.86g, Sodium: 914.26mg, Fiber: 9.98g

CONCLUSION

If you've bought a tagine for the first time and are wondering what to make in it, or you want an introduction to Moroccan main dishes, this book will give you the start you need.

All classic Moroccan recipes are tried and true favorites that are easy to prepare in traditional clay tagines or conventional cookware. Remember, clay cookware needs to be seasoned before its first use.

Made in the USA
Middletown, DE
08 October 2022